To Roy and Alice

With happy remembrance
of our days together in Cambridge
during the writing of this and a far
more important book.

Peter & Joan
March 1967

CHRISTIAN PRESENCE SERIES

EDITOR: M. A. C. WARREN

❖

Sweeter Than Honey

recently published by SCM Press Ltd

JEWISH PRAYER AND WORSHIP
An Introduction to Christians
WILLIAM W. SIMPSON

ON THE EIGHTFOLD PATH
Christian Presence Amid Buddhism
GEORGE APPLETON

JAPAN'S RELIGIOUS FERMENT
Christian Presence Amid Faiths Old and New
R. J. HAMMER

THE PRIMAL VISION
Christian Presence Amid African Religion
JOHN V. TAYLOR

INDIA'S RELIGIOUS FRONTIER
Christian Presence Amid Modern Hinduism
WILLIAM STEWART

PETER SCHNEIDER

Sweeter than Honey

>>><<<

*Christian Presence Amid
Judaism*

SCM PRESS LTD
BLOOMSBURY STREET LONDON

FIRST PUBLISHED 1966
© SCM PRESS LTD 1966
PRINTED IN GREAT BRITAIN BY
ROBERT CUNNINGHAM AND SONS LTD
ALVA, SCOTLAND

For
JEAN

General Introduction

>>>◆<<<

CHRISTIANS are being presented by the contemporary world with what is, in many ways, a unique opportunity of demonstrating the Gospel. Scarcely less unique is the opportunity being offered to them of discovering in a new and deeper way what that Gospel is. Those are large claims. Can they be justified?

What is this unique opportunity? At the very least it is the opportunity presented to Christians to demonstrate the fundamental truth of the Gospel that it is a universal message, whose relevance is not limited to any one culture, to any one system of thought, to any one pattern of activity. That is by no means the truism that it may appear to be. For more than four centuries the expansion of the Christian Church has coincided with the economic, political and cultural expansion of Western Europe. Viewed from the standpoint of the peoples of Asia, and to a growing extent from that of the peoples of Africa, this expansion has been an aggressive attack on their own way of life. Quite inevitably the Christian faith has for many in these lands been inextricably bound up with this Western aggression. But it has also to be admitted quite frankly that during these centuries the missionaries of the Christian Church have commonly assumed that Western civilization and Christianity were two aspects of the same gift which they were commissioned to offer to the rest of mankind.

This assumption was sometimes quite conscious and was explicitly stated. More often it was quite unconscious and would have been indignantly denied. But in neither case are we called upon to judge our fathers. Their sincerity can hardly be disputed. Their self-sacrificing devotion finds its monument today in the world-wide diffusion of the Christian faith, the existence, in almost every country of the world, of a community of Christians recognizably part of the Universal Church.

What we are called upon to recognize is that in the world of our time there is a widespread revolt against any form of domination by the West. Nations whose political independence was only achieved 'yesterday' or is only about to be achieved 'tomorrow' can be excused for having their own interpretation of the past, an interpretation unlikely to coincide with that which is prevalent in the West. This very waning of Western influence is in part our Christian opportunity. We are freer today than we have ever been to serve the Gospel without the risk of confusion between that Gospel and the 'power' of the West.

But that is not all. The peoples of Asia and Africa, in their revolt against domination by the West, are presenting a specific challenge to the Christian faith. In what does this consist?

There are three main ingredients in this challenge.

First there is a critical evaluation of the Christian religion which rejects it as something inherently Western, as something which fails to correspond to the *felt* needs of Asia and Africa. Christianity is, in such judgement,

8

altogether too Western in its character and in the form which it assumes in its local manifestations. This rejection is the more serious in that Asian and African peoples are themselves, like us in the West, confronted by the bewildering demands of the modern world. All the old landmarks are disappearing. Everywhere there is a desperate search for some inner basis of security, some inner assurance which can enable men and women to face the storm. In the sequel, particularly in Asia, but not only there, the peoples of these countries are seeking to find this psychic security by digging deep into their own past. This at once is an expression of their revolt against the West and one explanation of the resurgence of the great ethnic religions. Further to this it is to be noted that in a new way these ancient religions are becoming themselves missionary. No longer content to be on the defensive, they are offering themselves as answers to the questionings of mankind.

Here is a situation which is new. Only once before, and then in its earliest centuries, has the Christian Church had to face a comparable challenge to its claim to meet the deepest needs of man's heart and mind. The devotees of Mithras, the mystery cults of the Mediterranean world, the Gnostics in that earlier day were serious competitors with the message of the Gospel. Their appeal failed. There followed the long thousand years during which Europe was isolated from the rest of mankind and built for itself its own peculiar civilization. Then suddenly, drawing on its inner dynamism, a dynamism closely related to its faith, the European world overflowed its narrow boundaries and began its great expansion. For a time it appeared as if nothing

9

could arrest this expansion. It is of some importance to recognize that it is by no means certain that anything can! The scientific view of the world, with all its implications about human survival, is Western in origin. Communism and nationalism are Western concepts. It may well be doubted if anything can arrest the advance of all mankind towards something like a common civilization—if common destruction is avoided. Nevertheless there is, at the moment, a significant pause in the impetus of Western expansion in its Christian expression. The challenge to Christians is precisely this that the ethnic religions, as well as secularist philosophies of life, are offering themselves as the basis of the new world civilization. Both deny the relevance of Christianity.

The *second* challenge follows from the first. Can the Christian faith not only prove its ability to meet the deep human needs of our time but also make peoples of different cultural backgrounds feel at home in the new world? This is a more complex task than would appear. For it is part of our paradoxical situation that, at a moment when the world is becoming so obviously interdependent, every nation in it is seeking to assert its own independence. And religion and culture are the means by which independence is asserted. Has the Christian Church got a Gospel to meet this situation? We may put the question this way—can the Christians of the West accept the fact that the expression which Christianity will receive in its Asian and African forms may well be, almost certainly will be, in many respects very different indeed from what we know in the West? That again could be worded as follows—are we of the West prepared to trust the Holy Spirit to lead the Christians of Asia and

General Introduction

Africa, or must a controlling Western hand be permanently resting on the Ark of God? Let no one imagine that those questions will find an easy or unanimous response from Western Christians.

There remains a *third* challenge. The Christian Church has not yet seriously faced the theological problem of 'coexistence' with other religions. The very term seems to imply the acceptance of some limitation of the universal relevance of the Gospel. Can that be accepted? It can hardly be doubted that the answer must be 'no'. Are we then shut up to the alternative of what in some disguise or other must be an aggressive attack on the deeply held convictions of those who live by other faiths than our own?

This projected series of volumes has been designed to express a deliberate recognition of the challenges outlined above and to suggest that there is a way in which they can be met without any betrayal of the Gospel—indeed in deeper loyalty to that Gospel's real content.

First of the demands presented to us by this understanding of the contemporary world is a *glad* acceptance of the new situation in which the Christian faith can everywhere be distinguished from its past historical association with Western political, economic and cultural aggression. Here is the 'great new fact of our time', every whit as great a fact as the existence of the Church in every land. Here is our great new opportunity, even though it may well be an opportunity to witness through suffering. The Cross, after all, was not a symbol of imperial domination but of the *imperium* of sacrifice. The Christian faith has nothing to lose by suffering. In and through suffering it can perhaps speak home to the hearts and minds of suffering mankind better than in any other way.

Second of the demands upon us, to march with our gladness, is a deep humility, by which we remember that God has not left himself without witness in any nation at any time. When we approach the man of another faith than our own it will be in a spirit of expectancy to find how God has been speaking to him and what new understandings of the grace and love of God we may ourselves discover in this encounter.

Our first task in approaching another people, another culture, another religion, is to take off our shoes, for the place we are approaching is holy. Else we may find ourselves treading on men's dreams. More serious still, we may forget that God was here before our arrival. We have, then, to ask what is the authentic religious content in the experience of the Muslim, the Hindu, the Buddhist or whoever he may be. We may, if we have asked humbly and respectfully, still reach the conclusion that our brothers have started from a false premise and reached a faulty conclusion. But we must not arrive at our judgement from outside their religious situation. We have to try to sit where they sit, to enter sympathetically into the pains and griefs and joys of their history and see how those pains and griefs and joys have determined the premises of their argument. We have, in a word, to be 'present' with them.

This is what is meant by the title of this series—*Christian Presence* amid Islam, Hinduism, Buddhism. . . . This will not be an easy approach. But then the love of God is not easy.

The seventh volume in this series attempts, in some

ways, the most difficult task of all, an assessment of the Christian presence amid Judaism. That this task does not derive from the New Testament itself but from subsequent interpretation by Christians of the New Testament should be clear to anyone reading the Epistle to the Romans and in particular chapters 9-11. Nor, as the author of this volume makes clear, can anti-Jewish sentiments be derived from the Gospels. Even the pejorative use of the words 'Jews' in the Fourth Gospel must be read as descriptive of a controversy taking place within the people of Israel. Nothing is more clear from the New Testament than the fact that the Christian Church began amid Judaism and that only slowly and reluctantly did the New Israel separate from the Old Israel. Christ's lament over Jerusalem (Matthew 23. 37-39) and St Paul's cry in Romans 9. 2-3 strike two of the deepest notes in the New Testament.

In melancholy contrast with the sobriety and sorrow of the New Testament, and with its unquenchable hope that 'the whole of Israel will be saved' (Romans 11. 26 NEB), is the record of the Christian Church of the centuries that have followed down to our own day. Even the second session of the Second Vatican Council in the autumn of 1964 could not achieve *unanimity* in acquitting the Jewish people of the guilt of deicide, though it went further than any previous statement had done in repudiating the Church's record in the past.

A recent piece of historical detective writing by Miss M. D. Anderson in her book, *A Saint at Stake—The Strange Death of William of Norwich, 1144,* gives a vivid picture of twelfth-century England and of events in connection with the murder of a small boy which

13

became the pattern for a long chain of slanders against the Jewish people, and helped to create that deep suspicion in the European mind which made possible the Nazi holocaust. Despite the efforts of some mediaeval Popes to check the wild accusations brought against the Jews of the murder of Christian children in 'ritual sacrifices', the relentless preaching of anti-semitic hatred by too many churchmen created a mood among Christians which has been at once a denial of the fundamentals of the Christian Gospel and a formidable barrier to any reconciliation between Christians and Jews.

Mr Peter Schneider, in this volume, has with great skill, deep insight, wide knowledge and intimate sympathy penetrated to the heart of the great dilemma of Judaism and its age-long struggle to come to terms with the greatest Jew of all. The author offers no easy solution, and makes no presumptuous appeal to those of Jewish faith. Rather, and with justice, he summons Christians to the labour of understanding and the creative potentiality of penitence. Christian no less than Jew stands under the Cross to hear the words 'Father, forgive them, for they know not what they do'.

M. A. C. WARREN

Contents

Preface

>>>◆<<<

THE line of thought in the following chapters does not follow a natural progression and therefore some explanation is necessary. The Christian-Jewish relationship is unique but it is also tragic. For centuries it did not seem to dawn on Christians that there was something essentially wrong in the Christian attitude to and understanding of Jewry. The fearful holocaust of Nazi Germany has at last made Christians aware of this. It is at this point that the present study begins. The first chapter traces the story back to the Middle Ages while the second chapter begins with the New Testament and continues to the sources that directly influenced the mediaeval period. In the third chapter an attempt is made to see the historic relationship from the Jewish side. The ground having been cleared, the fourth chapter takes up a new theme of a glad encounter where Christians can learn from Judaism and discover it to be 'sweeter than honey'. The final chapter rather ambitiously attempts to delineate a possible new Christian-Jewish relationship freed from the misunderstandings of the past.

Any English writer using Hebrew terms is always faced with the intricate problem of how to transliterate Hebrew into English. It is impossible to be consistent, for there are bound to be quotations which employ different methods of transliteration. The old method attempted to express in English the peculiarities of Hebrew, so that even silent consonants were faithfully transliterated. *The New Jewish Encyclopedia* published by Behrman House (New York, 1962) greatly simplified all this by working on the basis that if the reader does not know Hebrew the important factor is to convey the sound of the Hebrew word without complicating the issue by indicating in English how the word is actually written in Hebrew. In Israel this phonetic tendency has been taken even further and, one might add, with great success. Wherever possible this phonetic principle has been followed, though at times, as for instance in the word 'Torah', the prevailing English usage has been kept out of deference to English conservatism in spelling.

My indebtedness to others will be evident on every page. I am particularly indebted to Dr James Parkes (and his wife Dorothy) for the most generous help and advice he has given me at every stage of the writing of this book. My debt to him and to his generous facility in the use of his library at Barley (it has now been removed to Southampton University) is immense. It would, however, be unfair to hold him responsible for the views expressed in the following pages. I am equally indebted to the General Editor of this series. Were it not for his trust and understanding this study would never have been undertaken or ever brought to a conclusion. The Reverend Harry Ellison very kindly read the typescript and made many pertinent suggestions. I have been in his debt for many years and have often benefited from his candid advice. For the privilege of living in Israel and the impetus that this has given me to think out what is involved by a

Preface

'Christian Presence' in this new and exciting centre of Jewry, I am indebted to a great multitude but in particular I must single out Professor Zwi Werblowsky, whose incisive penetration has often dispelled my rather naive thinking.

I am also grateful to my diocesan, Archbishop MacInnes of Jerusalem, for kindly granting me leave of absence from Israel for the supposed quiet of Cambridge. In that beautiful place I am further indebted to the Censor and Fellows of Fitzwilliam House for the generous way in which they received me back into the fold. Also my thanks are due to the Chief Clerk and his staff, Mrs Elizabeth Turner and Miss Judith Moore for their efficient help in the typing of a very difficult MS. My indebtedness is yet further increased as the first MS (the full typescript is available in the Parkes Library) had to be considerably shortened and a more popular approach effected. This accounts for the scarcity of footnotes and quotations, but it is hoped that the more detailed reference to books in Appendix II will somewhat mitigate this deficiency and also be of help to further reading. I am most grateful to Mrs Lapidot, Mrs Boin and Miss Collins, who kindly helped in all the necessary retyping. To my wife, who also struggled with my MS, I am indebted in more ways than I care to mention.

PETER SCHNEIDER

Jerusalem, Israel
December 1965

19

1

Christianity and Anti-Semitism

>>>◆<<<

Since the fourth century after Christ, there have been three
anti-Jewish policies: conversion, expulsion and annihilation.
The second appeared as an alternative to the first and the
third emerged as an alternative to the second.[1]

MODERN Israel, viewed from any angle, is a most unusual place. It has been described as a pressure cooker of
cultures and civilizations, a small area where the past and
present are pressed together into a living form. So you
may travel the nearly two hundred miles from the biblical landmarks of Dan to Beersheba in an air-conditioned
bus of the main Israeli bus company, *Egged*. On the way
you cannot help but pass a few of the more than two
hundred agricultural settlements known as *kibbutzim*.
Many signposts will indicate some new town or settlement characterized by its tall co-operative flats known as
shikunim, while others will point to many an ancient *tell*,
such as Meggido, where the good King Josiah met his
death at the hands of the Egyptians in 608 BC.

Haifa is a modern seaport town with all the commercial trimmings that one associates with an up-to-date
European port. It is only fifteen miles from the ancient

[1] Raoul Hilberg, *The Destruction of the European Jews* (W. H. Allen,
London, 1961), p. 3.

sea fortress of Acre. *En route* one is not only over-shadowed by Mount Carmel, where Elijah battled for Israel's belief in one God, but pressing in on one is a whole belt of industrial and scientific factory plants that has been termed 'Israel's Steel City'. In this part of Israel—and stretching further north—live most of the quarter-million Israeli Arabs. Their way of life is rapidly changing yet in some of their Galilean villages one is still very close to the atmosphere of New Testament times.

The majority Jewish population of close on to two and a half million is far from uniform. In the all-Jewish town of Tel Aviv, the metropolis of Israel, there are Jews from the Yemen whose mother tongue is Arabic mingling with Jews from every part of Europe and the Americas. Today, less than half a century after the recognition of Hebrew as one of the official languages of mandate Palestine and after only eighteen years of its acceptance as the first language of the land, Hebrew has undoubtedly established itself as the predominant language of Israel. Much of this is due to the success of the *Ulpanim*, adult language schools, where Hebrew is taught in Hebrew. It could hardly be otherwise in a class that possesses no common language and it is, after all, only taking advantage of the way in which we all learn our first language. Such resourcefulness, plus a pulsating vitality, characterizes the entire Israeli scene. Not only is the average Israeli hard-working, many holding down two jobs and some even three, not only is there great experiment in agriculture, industry, and technological expertise (Israel is supplying many of the new African states with technicians), but also in the area of higher learning the impossible is attempted. There are at present three universities and two highly advanced scientific institutes, and yet another university is being planned. There is as yet no television, but art and music flourish. Besides several art colonies, there is an entire artist community living and working in their own village of Ein Hod on Mount Carmel. Music enjoys the kind of popular support that is associated in Britain with the Proms and Sir Malcolm Sargent. To all this, in the eighteenth year of its independence Israel has added a National Museum in Jerusalem that has been acclaimed as a cultural centre of world importance and can boast among its varied treasures a significant unit of Billy Rose's most modern sculpture and a fantastic mausoleum, the Shrine of the Book, that houses some of the renowned Dead Sea Scrolls.

It has often been questioned how Israel can afford such cultural luxuries when at the same time it has to guard some six hundred and twenty miles of frontier with unfriendly neighbours. There is no simple answer, not even a straightforward negative, for, difficult as life is, Israel is not on the verge of economic bankruptcy. This modern state, whose first university was founded almost a quarter of a century before its own independence was achieved, has grown to recognize that its resources and responsibilities stretch far beyond the confines of a modern nation. They reach back and forward to encompass the demands of the unique qualities of the Jewish people as it has emerged from its own rugged history. That history involves a miracle of survival which is today summed up in Israel's resolute determination to be and to continue to be. This renewal of the Jewish people's historic will to survive challenges the modern state to face all those forces that have for so long, and most recently in Hitler's

Europe, worked for its destruction and annihilation. All this became dramatically real in the Jerusalem of 1962, in the bullet-proof dock of the improvised courtroom at the Beit Ha-Am (The House of the People) where Adolf Eichmann was obliged to listen day after day as Israel's Attorney-General, Gideon Hausner, recounted the awesome details of Hitler's final solution. It seemed then that not only the man who had callously worked to annihilate five million, one hundred and one thousand Jews, but all that is summed up in that twelve lettered term anti-semitism, was on trial in the capital of Israel. The weeks of the trial were a taut and terrible experience that strained the very nerves of the nation. For many of the survivors of the concentration camps it meant sleepless nights; for the young Israeli it was a rude reminder that such atrocities had been successfully perpetrated against his European kith and kin; and for the Christian present in all this it was a day of judgement.

Christians generally and particularly those in contact with Jews were not unaware that there was some connection between Christendom and anti-semitism but there is a built-in psychological reaction that makes most of us evade culpability for the death of so many as *five million, one hundred and one thousand*. Yet what was being re-enacted in a courtroom in Jerusalem in 1962 somehow forced the question '*Is it I?*' For most of us following the trial at the time there was a sense of great relief when Adolf Eichmann refused to swear on the New Testament. One Jewish commentator pertinently observed that there were after all limits to even the most nominal type of Christianity. Adolf Eichmann had gone beyond that limit. Certainly there were diabolical and

24

anti- and post-Christian forces at work in Hitler's final solution, but there were religious roots, or to be more precise, Christian roots out of which the full-grown plant with all its ugly manifestations grew.

The scope of this book precludes a thorough-going history of anti-semitism, but its motivation demands at least a candid analysis of what this evil is and how far we as Christians are involved in it. While no historical outline is here attempted, we have continually to allow the facts to confront us and to ask, 'What does it all amount to, and how am *I* as a Christian involved?' The courtroom in Jerusalem may well be the point at which our conscience is ignited, but it is a mere beginning of our awareness of a full history of attitudes and deeds that finally culminated in what was openly exposed and condemned in Jerusalem. We need now—however rapidly—to retrace our steps so that at least we may understand the rise of the movement which gave an age-long anti-Jewish prejudice a new impetus and a new name.

In a brilliant essay published in 1911, in the eleventh edition of the *Encyclopaedia Britannica*, Lucien Wolf gives us an anatomy of political and pre-Nazi anti-semitism that is at once restrained and candid. The Christian will read with great relief of the political and economic causes of modern anti-semitism, but let us be warned that our relief, such as it is, can only be short-lived. Lucien Wolf comes to the conclusion that 'anti-Semitism is thus exclusively a question of European politics, and its origin is to be found, not in the long struggle between Europe and Asia or between the Church and Synagogue, which filled so much of ancient and mediaeval history, but in the social conditions resulting from the emancipation of the

25

Jews in the middle of the nineteenth century'. These words by themselves might lead us to inadequate conclusions. Their great value is that they call our attention to the new form that the age-old Jew hatred took in the new world of Bismarck's Germany. The modern movement arose from the political and economic opportunism in Germany of the eighteen-seventies. The need for cementing political unity after territorial unity has been achieved is well known, and to this we should add Bismarck's search for sufficient economic expertise to make smooth the transfer from an essentially feudal society to one of modern commerce. At this point we can discern the beginnings of economic and political failure. Instead of searching out a sure road towards political unity and economic stability, the politicians thought that they had found a short cut in the fabrication of a racist ideology which would unite all Germans and achieve prosperity, and all at the small expense of the expulsion of the alien Jews. It seemed too tempting to the politicians and economists of the day that in their very midst was a differing minority which had already in the past been used as a whipping boy, so that when such economic and political theorizing broke down in actual practice, the Jews were a handy scapegoat to divert attention from the inherent weakness of the ideology itself. This political pattern can and does repeat itself. Its outward form and complexity varies considerably but the fundamental need for a scapegoat and an enemy remains constant. It is perhaps because modern anti-semitism has such a fundamental ideological fallacy at its point of departure from mediaeval Jew hatred that it can never be dispelled by merely attacking its grandiose superstructure, without showing

26

up these foundations which have time and again been proved to be made of sand.

Once we have seen the political and economic foundations of anti-semitism for what they are, the actual superstructure, the history of lies about the character of the Jewish people, is easy to demolish. It was precisely because the early anti-semites started from such a fictitious hypothesis that they found it necessary not only to use the Jews as a scapegoat, but also to revive the ancient and malignant prejudice against them, in order to bolster up their case. These accusations have much in common with the mediaeval prejudice and superstition, but the only relation to the actual character of the Jewish people was a gross caricature which appealed to what people liked to think of a differing minority but which could not stand up to the scrutiny of reality. This has been demonstrated again and again. Those accusations affecting personal conduct, particularly concerning commercial and political integrity, aimed to prove that the Jew is a parasite and basically unpatriotic. Other assaults included the whole of the Jewish people as essentially the enemy of western civilization and the plotters of world domination. Both these types of offensive reached a point of *reductio ad absurdum*, as is evident in the Dreyfus Affair and the *Protocols of the Elders of Zion*. And yet the seriousness with which both were treated shows how well the anti-semites had succeeded in drawing attention away from their fundamental hypothesis and how prone society is to believe a fabricated evil of a minority if this is repeated long and hard enough.

There have been thousands of libellous accusations against individual Jews, but the value of the Dreyfus

Affair is that it showed up the unscrupulousness of the anti-semites who thought nothing of forging documents and impugning even a noted member of the hated minority although he was part of the army establishment. It brought France to the verge of civil war and because the Roman Catholic Church was so heavily involved it helped to sever its tenuous hold as the established religion of France. Although it is evident that the forgeries behind the affair were exposed early in the twelve-year struggle, it yet proved extremely difficult to exonerate Alfred Dreyfus. Even when he was finally vindicated in 1906 and received the Order of Merit, it was not the death blow to the anti-semites. Only one aspect of the anti-semitic superstructure had been demolished. However disgraceful the Dreyfus Affair it pales in comparison with the evil machinations behind the so-called *Protocols of the Elders of Zion*.[1] This was to be the final proof that the Jews had always been a common enemy. Indeed, they had been planning for a whole millennium the complete overthrow of the Christian West in order that they might rule the world. It sounds fantastic, but then so also is the actual document of the *Protocols*. Even a cursory glance at these *Protocols* would make one wonder how any intelligent person could have taken them seriously. The fact that they were even considered as a genuine Jewish plot is far more serious than the supposed portent of the document itself. Although it was exposed by a correspondent of the London *Times* in 1921, it was once more

[1] *The Protocols* were first published in the last decade of the nineteenth century in Russia, but attracted little attention until the eve of the Russian revolution in 1917. They were then used to prove that the Jews were on the Bolshevik side and so caused the death of hundreds of Russian Jews.

28

brought up in Switzerland and finally condemned by the Canton court of Bern in 1935 which not only exposed the *Protocols* as a forgery but further declared them to be obscene literature. All this (and much more that has been written on the subject) underlines how much the mediaeval superstitions concerning the Jews lingered on into the present day and is directly related to the gross national self-delusion regarding the Jews forced on the German people by Hitler. Certainly, Streicher's periodical *Der Stürmer*, published in the time of Nazi Germany, is a development of phantasy and obscenity on lines similar to the *Protocols*.

Both the above instances were external to Germany, and it is a fact of history that in the number of its Jewish victims Czarist Russia far outdid pre-Hitler Germany. A closer examination of these facts shows that, as far as Russia was concerned, it was the continuation of mediaeval persecution, made possible by still largely prevailing mediaeval conditions, together with an infusion of the new political anti-semitism, that resulted in the notorious pogroms at the turn of the century. The new element in nineteenth-century anti-semitism, as we have already indicated, is its racio-political slant combined with an evil past which makes it, in Raoul Hilberg's phrase, 'a cyclical phenomenon'. Historians of anti-semitism have often pondered the reason why Germany became the centre of modern Jew hatred. Was it perhaps because there was a special pre-conditioning in Germany? This very question has made people think back to the great formative thinker and reformer Martin Luther. Certainly, it is not difficult to find anti-Jewish statements in Luther's writings. The very title of his fiercest tract in this direction, *The Jews and their Lies*, written in 1543, was ready-made material for modern anti-semitic propaganda. There are, however, extenuating circumstances which somewhat mitigate Luther's guilt. At the commencement of his reformation Luther had some kind things (for his day!) to say about the Jews. It was wrong, he maintained, to use force in order to convert. Indeed, Christ's law of love was a much more appropriate tool. In other words, persuasion and not coercion should be used. Luther at first even admitted that one cannot blame the Jews for not accepting Christianity because, 'the papists have so demeaned themselves that a good Christian would rather be a Jew than one of them, and a Jew would rather be a sow than a Christian. What good can we do to the Jews when we constrain them, malign them, and hate them as dogs? When we deny them work and force them to usury, how can that help? We should use toward the Jews not the pope's but Christ's law of love. If some are stiff-necked, what does that matter? We are not all good Christians.'[1]

What then accounts for his later attitude? Among many possibilities the following at least partially help to account for Luther's change. (i) Luther was a flamboyant personality and is known to have said strange things at moments of pressure. (ii) Luther had at first entertained the hope that once his reformation had effected a clean-up of the faith, the Jews would be only too ready to embrace Christianity. In this he was greatly disappointed. When Luther tried to convince certain rabbis of the truth of Christianity he found to his dismay that, far from being convinced, they tried to convince him of the truth of

[1] Quoted by Roland Bainton, *Here I Stand* (Hodder and Stoughton, London, 1951), p. 379.

Judaism. (iii) We need to recognize that in the first in-stance Luther's so-called 'new attitude' to the Jews was only a by-product of his fury against the papists. When he was disappointed in the Jews' refusal to be converted and pressed by a Judaic movement among Christians in Bohemia he simply reverted to the old mediaeval pre-judice.

It is to the great shame of Protestants that, at a time when so many of the abuses of the Church were put to an end, those concerning the Jews were perpetuated. It is at this point that Luther's guilt is undeniable. His unfortunate writings on the Jews are certainly not basic to his religion or central to his thought. To make them out to be so is to caricature him. It is only because of the stature and influence of Luther that the anti-semites troubled to dig out writings that would support their ideology. None the less, our involvement as Protestants in anti-semitism was clearly written in 1543!

But Protestants are also Christians and, as such, our involvement goes back to the mediaeval Jew hatred which Luther so unfortunately helped to perpetuate. An historical outline of the Church's treatment of the Jews in the Middle Ages would involve us in nothing less than an outline of the whole history of that period. For the immediate purpose of exposing the roots of mediaeval Jew hatred, it may be permissible merely to spotlight certain critical events which illustrate and typify the Church's treatment of the Jews. We need, however, to remind ourselves that this kind of selection all too easily leads to a distortion of the total situation. So in the maze of legislation that affects the Jews and in the available detail of their treatment by Christians, it would be possible to view the period from the first Crusade in the eleventh century to the Spanish Inquisition in the fourteenth, as a continuing acceleration leading to the Russian pogroms of the late nineteenth century and the Nazi holocaust of our own time. It would likewise be possible to draw a picture depicting the good relations which existed between many Jews and Christians during this period (this is particularly true of the six hundred years leading up to the eleventh century), and to demonstrate that despite certain restrictive legislation and outbreaks of mob hysteria there was also such protective legislation as the *Constitutio Pro Judaeis* issued in 1120 and reinforced by no less than ten Popes by 1250. Much could be said about the part played by the papacy in the mistreatment of Jews. It is also true that the papacy not infrequently attempted to protect the Jews from mob hysteria and to clear them from such superstitious accusations as the poisoning of wells and ritual murder. The truth does not lie in a compromise but in the greater complexity involved in following both lines of approach.

To understand this complexity we need to take note of the legislation that preceded the mediaeval period which commenced, in fact, at the moment of the Church's assumption of political power with the rise of Constantine at the beginning of the fourth century. Even a cursory glance at Raoul Hilberg's table of 'Canonical and Nazi Anti-Jewish Measures' (reproduced at the end of this chapter) will indicate that the predominant note in anti-Jewish legislation up to the sixth century was of an exclusive character—it attempted to shut the Jews up and thus segregate them from the majority of Christians among whom they lived. Hard as this legislation certainly was (segregation usually attracts to itself more evil bed-fellows than itself—it does not easily abide alone), its effect was at least limited. More serious were the reasons which brought such legislation into being. Before attempting to enumerate them it is instructive to note that the persecution of Jews on a large scale can be said to begin several centuries later with the Crusades and after that grew more and more frequent, rising in ferocity at the time of the Black Death, in the mid-fourteenth century, and the upsurge of religious fanaticism in the Spanish Inquisition.

We may note that there was a considerable time-lag between the commencement of the Church's anti-Jewish legislation in the fourth century and the outbreak of a full-scale persecution in the eleventh century. During the Roman Empire Jews and Christians were given very similar treatment except that after the second century, when the Jews were no longer a potential political danger, they were treated with less severity. What made the restrictive Christian anti-Jewish legislation from the fourth century onwards so harmful was that it was supported by an image of the Jews which the early Church had developed in her polemic with Judaism, and which we find already fully formed in the writings of St Chrysostom. This degraded image of Judaism needed time to seep into the general Christian consciousness, but when it had done so it became henceforth unshakable. So the Jew, who first of all only resisted Christian pressure to be assimilated in conversion, was soon seen as a stubborn heretic and from there it was not difficult to connect him with the father of all heresy, the devil. Now that the Jews had been safely excluded from Christian society, it

33

was easy for this theological creation of a Jewish monster to develop into an image applicable to the whole of Jewry. This accumulative derogation of both Jews and Judaism and the way in which it was linked to well-known images of evil and superstition accounts for the formation and development of the specific mediaeval anti-Jewish accusations.

It is certainly extremely difficult to divide the ever increasing accusations against the Jews in this era into water-tight compartments of theological, superstitious, economic and political origin; yet all these factors are present in the mediaeval accusations. At the risk of over-simplification it is possible to trace a line of development and so to indicate how the Jews, who since the fourth century and before had been castigated as guilty of dei-cide, should at the time of the Crusades (more or less a Holy War against infidels) be viewed as part of the infidel army dwelling in the very heart of Christendom. We have already seen that through their resistance to con-version the Jews were associated with the cause of all unbelief, the devil. Given the suspicion of a minority which was already present and the gross superstition of the time, it is not difficult to see how the Jews at a time of plague came to be accused as 'poisoners of wells', a charge levelled against them at the time of the Black Death and which attempted to fix the responsibility of this and other plagues upon them. From this position, it was but a small step to the persistent accusations of deicide, 'ritual murder' and 'profanation of the Host'. To this was added the additional accusation of 'black magic' which was applied quite indiscriminately to the classical expression of Jewish mysticism known as the Kabbala, and the impugning of the normative literature as expressed in the Talmud as being the main source of a profane attack upon Christianity—fit only to be burned!

It is not pleasant to review the mediaeval development of Jew hatred seen in such specific accusations as poisoning wells, ritual murder, deicide and profanation of the Host, to which we must add unsociableness and usury, but it does demonstrate that political and economic considerations were interwoven with theological and superstitious factors. From this, two deductions would seem to be permissible. (i) There is a striking resemblance between the superstitious anti-Jewish accusations arising in the Middle Ages and some of the pre-Constantine pagan accusations against Christianity, namely that Christians practised cannibalism in the celebration of the Eucharist, that they were atheists, haters of men, and incendiarists. These wholly pagan inventions were, to our shame, covered in a veneer of Christian terminology and reapplied to the Jews. (ii) The extension of the Church's conflict with the Jews into the political and economic realm underlines how greatly modern anti-semitism was built upon mediaeval Jew hatred.

It may be that at this point we are tempted to think that this sorry image of the Jews was only true of Christendom as a whole and hardly applicable to the individual Christian at that time. It is also possible to maintain that several popes during this period tried to foster a more enlightened attitude to the Jews. The tragedy is that the Church's vituperation of Judaism had become such an integral part of Christian teaching that not even specific alleviating rules of the popes had much effect on the conscience of the faithful in their attitude to the Jews.

35

Count Coudenhove-Kalergi gives a telling example of a pious knight who is drawn to follow the dictates of his conscience rather than obey the specific rulings of the pope as affecting the baptism of Jewish children. He relates:

Let us imagine a devout Christian mediaeval knight in whose power a Jewish child accidentally found itself. He is tempted to baptize this child and thus wrest it from its parents for ever. At the same time, however, he is also aware of the fact that such an action was strictly forbidden by the Pope and that he was liable to be punished for it. What would, in the opinion of the reader, have been the outcome of the struggle in the breast of the knight? In one hundred, perhaps ninety-nine cases, the knight would have argued as follows: 'As matters stand this Jewish child has come into my power. It is not an accident but a Divine indication. If I baptize this child, our Holy Church gains a believer, Heaven has one more saint, and I will save a soul which will now belong to God. It is impossible that God will condemn me to eternal punishment for bringing Him in this manner the soul of a child. His parents to be sure will die of grief but what do I care for the grief of deicides and enemies of our Church. Of course, I am committing a sin in disobeying the express command of the Pope, but I am convinced that this sin will be easily forgiven unto me. Therefore let us baptize this child in God's name for it is quite impossible that I should one day be thrown into hell because I had brought the Church and God a human soul even if I did it in an unlawful way.'[1]

[1] Count Richard Coudenhove-Kalergi, *Anti-Semitism throughout the Ages* (Eng. trans. by A. S. Rappoport, Hutchinson, London, 1935), p. 99. (The German original appeared in 1901, entitled *Das Wesen des Anti-semitismus*.) Behind this study lies a lifelong inquiry into the origins of anti-semitism. It is particularly significant in that its author is the first Christian scholar to suggest a direct connection between the 'Anti-Judaism' of the early Christian Church and later mediaeval Jew hatred and modern anti-semitism.

Christianity and Anti-Semitism

This example is not as archaic or imaginary as it may at first appear. Ironically in 1965, when no Christian church in Israel (or outside) practises forced baptisms of minors or adults, the Israeli Knesset (parliament) found it necessary to introduce legislation against the conversion of minors. Certainly one cannot judge the mediaeval practice of forced baptisms with the yardstick of twentieth century religious liberty, but the truth is that this practice lingered on far beyond the confines of the mediaeval period. It is an injustice that has penetrated deep into the Jewish consciousness.

Before proceeding in the next chapter to an outline of the Christian-Jewish polemic which leads up to the image of Judaism drawn by St Chrysostom, which we have taken to be the point of departure for the mediaeval derogation of Jewry and Judaism, we must face once again its ultimate development in such a way as will prevent us fron over-simplifying the evil of anti-semitism and our own sin and involvement. True, the first signpost on the way of this development may only be marked contempt on the religious level, but we soon come across the rest, superstitious prejudice, economic opportunism, racist ideology and then suddenly we turn a sharp corner and there is a steep descent paved with ruthless technical efficiency. We are at the gates of Hell! This is what happened to European Jewry who experienced such torments of destruction in twelve horrific years from 1933 to 1945, beside which all the misery and torment of centuries of tribulation pale in comparison.

Even at this point our disquiet is not at an end. Christian shame increases as we remember the extent to which the Christian Church kept silent. To our great relief there were individual Christians who did protest and resist, and among them, thank God, were German Christians, yet only in Holland and in Denmark was there anything like national resistance that was supported by the Church as a whole. Surely the Church should have taken more note of these Christians who stood in the forefront of the battle. Some account of them has been taken, but not to the measure of their deeds. It is in fact the Jewish people rather than the Christian Church who has honoured their memory as is evident in a special plantation of trees dedicated to the Righteous Gentiles in the Holocaust Memorial known as Yad-Vashem, on the Theodore Herzl Hill outside Jerusalem.

Can any Christian now say another word in the presence of a Jew? There is here very little for our comfort, and yet there is no other starting point for a 'Christian presence amid Judaism' than a genuine sense of unease as we face the Christian roots of anti-semitism. There are Christians today who openly admit that they have grown rather weary of this twelve-lettered subject. Surely enough has already been written and spoken on anti-semitism, and is there not a danger that if too much is said the tide of sympathy that has welled up on behalf of the Jews might well revert to one of suspicion that after all there must be something wrong with the Jews? This is a real danger, one that has been recognized by Jews as well as Christians, and it must place a certain restraint on what is spoken or written. Mere pious horror is certainly out of place.

So far it has only been possible to indicate the rough outlines of the complex histories of mediaeval Jew hatred and modern anti-semitism. We have tried not to cover up the approach or to stop short of the utter horror at the end of this road. If we have been somewhat shocked by facing Hitler's so-called final solution, then let us remember that the more we are aware of what caused it to happen and where it all led to, the less we shall be tempted to dismiss it as an outworn evil. That is why we need to inquire still deeper into 'how it all began', so that we might at least know the full extent of our involvement as Christians. The need for penitence thus realized will be the first intimation that a 'Christian presence amid Judaism' is a genuine possibility.

CANONICAL AND NAZI ANTI-JEWISH MEASURES[1]

CANONICAL LAW	NAZI MEASURE
Prohibition of intermarriage and of sexual intercourse between Christians and Jews, Synod of Elvira, 306	Law for the protection of German Blood and Honor, 15 September 1935 (RGBl I, 1146)
Jews and Christians not permitted to eat together, Synod of Elvira, 306	Jews barred from dining cars (Transport Minister to Interior Minister, 30 December 1939, Document NG-3995)
Jews not allowed to hold public office, Synod of Clermont, 535	Law for the Re-establishment of the Professional Civil Service, 7 April 1933 (RGBl I, 175)
Jews not allowed to employ Christian servants or possess Christian slaves, 3rd Synod of Orleans, 538	Law for the Protection of German Blood and Honor, 15 September 1935 (RGBl I, 1146)
Jews not permitted to show themselves in the streets during Passion Week, 3rd Synod of Orleans, 538	Decree authorizing local authorities to bar Jews from the streets on certain days (i.e. Nazi holidays), 3 December 1938 (RGBl I, 1676)

[1] Reproduced from Raoul Hilberg, *The Destruction of the European Jews* (sponsored by the Frank and Janina Petschek Foundation, published by Quadrangle Books, Chicago, and W. H. Allen, London, 1961), pp. 5-6.

CANONICAL LAW	NAZI MEASURE
Burning of the Talmud and other books, 12th Synod of Toledo, 681	Book burnings in Nazi Germany
Christians not permitted to patronize Jewish doctors, Trulanic Synod, 692	Decree of 25 July 1938 (RGBl I, 969)
Christians not permitted to live in Jewish homes, Synod of Narbonne, 1050	Directive by Göring providing for concentration of Jews in houses, 28 December 1938 (Bormann to Rosenberg, 17 January 1939, PS-69)
Jews obliged to pay taxes for support of the Church to the same extent as Christians, Synod of Gerona, 1078	The 'Sozialausgleichsabgabe' which provided that Jews pay a special income tax in lieu of donations for Party purposes imposed on Nazis, 24 December 1940 (RGBl I, 1666)
Prohibition of Sunday work, Synod of Szabolcs, 1092	
Jews not permitted to be plaintiffs, or witnesses against Christians in the Courts, 3rd Lateran Council, 1179, Canon 26	Proposal by the Party Chancellery that Jews not be permitted to institute civil suits, 9 September 1942 (Bormann to Justice Ministry, 9 September 1942, NG-151)
Jews not permitted to withhold inheritance from descendants who had accepted Christianity, 3rd Lateran Council, 1179, Canon 26	Decree empowering the Justice Ministry to void wills offending the 'sound judgement of the people', 31 July 1938 (RGBl I, 937)
The marking of Jewish clothes with a badge, 4th Lateran Council, 1215, Canon 68 (copied from the legislation by Caliph Omar II [634-44], who had decreed that Christians wear blue belts and Jews yellow belts)	Decree of 1 September 1941 (RGBl I, 547)
Construction of new synagogues prohibited, Council of Oxford, 1222	Destruction of synagogues in entire Reich, 10 November 1938 (Heydrich to Göring, 11 November 1938, PS-3058)

40

Christianity and Anti-Semitism

CANONICAL LAW	NAZI MEASURE
Christians not permitted to attend Jewish ceremonies, Synod of Vienna, 1267	Friendly relations with Jews prohibited, 24 October 1941 (Gestapo directive, L-15)
Jews not permitted to dispute with simple Christian people about the tenets of the Catholic religion, Synod of Vienna, 1267	
Compulsory ghettos, Synod of Breslau, 1267	Order by Heydrich, 21 September 1939 (PS-3363)
Christians not permitted to sell or rent real estate to Jews, Synod of Ofen, 1279	Decree providing for compulsory sale of Jewish real estate, 3 December 1938 (RGBl I, 1709)
Adoption by a Christian of the Jewish religion or return by a baptized Jew to the Jewish religion defined as a heresy, Synod of Mainz, 1310	Adoption by a Christian of the Jewish religion places him in jeopardy of being treated as a Jew. Decision by Oberlandesgericht Königsberg, 4th Zivilsenat, 26 June 1942 (*Die Judenfrage* [*Vertrauliche Beilage*], 1 November 1942, pp. 82-83)
Sale or transfer of Church articles to Jews prohibited, Synod of Lavour, 1368	
Jews not permitted to act as agents in the conclusion of contracts between Christians, especially marriage contracts, Council of Basel, 1434, Sessio XIX	Decree of 6 July 1938 providing for liquidation of Jewish real estate agencies, brokerage agencies and marriage agencies catering to non-Jews (RGBl I, 823)
Jews not permitted to obtain academic degrees, Council of Basel, 1434, Sessio XIX	Law against Overcrowding of German Schools and Universities, 25 April 1933 (RGB I, 225)

2

Whose Bible?

>>>◆<<<

What advantage then hath the Jew? . . . Much every way:
chiefly because that unto them were committed the oracles of
God . . . to whom pertaineth the adoption and the glory, and
the covenants and the giving of the law, and the service of
God and the promises. . . . *Romans 3.1-2; 9.4*

. . . do not imitate certain people by heaping sin after sin
upon yourselves and saying: 'Their covenant is ours also.'
Ours in deed; but in the end they lost it without more ado
when Moses had already received it . . .Moses understood:
he flung the two tablets out of his hands and their covenant
was shattered, that the covenant of the beloved Jesus might
be sealed in our heart. . . . *Epistle of Barnabas 4.6-8*

They are laid up in your (Jewish) scriptures, or rather not
in yours but in ours. *Justin, Dialogue 29.2*

IT is an unforgettable experience to travel on an Arab bus
from Haifa to Nazareth. It is an uphill journey and at
times spiral in ascent, yet the thirty miles, with numerous
stops and to the accompaniment of radio music all man-
aged by a single driver-conductor, are achieved in just
under one hour! If one's Arabic is good enough one would
also hear much politics. There are complaints about the
government, questions as to the future of the Arab
minority in the so-called triangle of which Nazareth is
the capital. It would be idle to pretend that all is well in

Whose Bible?

Nazareth. Naturally enough this one and only Israel town with an all-Arab population and its surrounding Arab villages feels keenly its isolation from its own kith and kin in the great Arab world of the rest of the Middle East from which in its present location within Israel it is almost totally cut off. The Israeli government has done much to relieve the situation. It is striving both to integrate the Arab minority into the common life of the state and also to preserve its ethnic identity. So the government has subsidized Arab housing and education, initiated Arab-Jewish youth clubs, guaranteed seven seats in the Knesset and a regular Arabic broadcast as part of the Kol Yisrael (national broadcasting company) service. Yet there have been mistakes and certain ambiguities remain.

The two most resented government policies are the compulsory sale of land (Israel has no alternative with its immigration rate but to exploit and develop the land, while the Arabs are bound to prefer their family plots to monetary compensation) and the exclusion of Arabs from most scientific jobs. For the up-and-coming Israeli Arab this is a continuous frustration, for the Israeli government it is a matter of security. It is at once a tragedy and a dilemma. No doubt the government could do more, but the only real solution of the anxieties and tensions of the Israeli Arabs is a peace settlement between Israel and her Arab neighbours. In the meantime, however little the Christian Church can do (and it is very little!) she cannot aspire to anything less than the complex task of peace-making. At the present, this may be limited to the exacting backroom work of a mere preparation in understanding. Always that will involve much listening and sometimes a readiness to be misunderstood by both sides. In all this complexity there is the added irritation that the political tension between Israel and her Arab neighbours has tended to intrude into the Church's attempt to renovate her relationship with Jewry and Judaism.

And so we return to our bus conversation. Politics, did we say? Yes, that is right but in the autumn of 1964 the interest suddenly switched to what the Vatican Council was saying about the Jews.[1] Time and again one could hear—'They (that is the Council Fathers) are changing the Gospel.' Why? Because 'they have cleared the Jews from deicide'. This question of deicide, which a decade ago was only known to scholars and anti-semitic writers, has suddenly reappeared and become a common talking-point in Israel. The Christian Church will not make peace by giving way to political pressure. It is of little use to ask whether it is expedient to press at this time such far-reaching questions as 'Does the New Testament accuse the Jews of deicide?' It is a Christian hope that there will be peace in the Middle East and this certainly involves being sensitive to the Arab Palestinian tragedy. However, it is a false short cut to that hope and aspiration to avoid facing that age-old Christian accusation against the Jews. This means that we cannot stop short of asking whether there are anti-semitic tendencies within the New Testament itself.

It will at once be evident that this is a far harder question for Christians to answer than anything we have so far faced in the first chapter, and that in itself is a sufficient reason why it should not be avoided. It is of

[1] See Appendix I for the Council's statement together with a recent declaration on this issue by the Archbishop of Canterbury.

course a gross anachronism to use the term anti-semitism in relation to the New Testament, but when we are tracing roots it is hardly possible to stop short of these primary sources. It is perhaps well to warn ourselves that certain statements in Isaiah have been used, or we should rather say misused, for anti-semitic purposes; indeed in one of the harshest words of St Paul against the Jews (Acts 28.25-28) he quotes from Isaiah. There is however a distinction in what Isaiah says about his fellow country-men and co-religionists from what the New Testament and subsequent Christian writers say about the Jews. Isaiah writes wholly within the Jewish community and his words are nothing else but healthy self-criticism, and almost the same can be said for the Synoptic Gospels. But for the New Testament as a whole it is somewhat differ-ent, as it is a time of transition, for a new community is emerging but it is not as yet sharply differentiated from the parent community. However, soon after New Testa-ment times the Jewish and Christian communities steadily moved towards being mutually exclusive. An easy illus-tration to hand may be the differences expressed by speakers at a wholly Anglican gathering like the Toronto Congress of 1963 where it might be permissible to indulge in some fairly harsh judgements on Anglicanism. This could hardly be viewed as anti-Anglican but rather as healthy self-criticism. The position alters considerably when one considers for example what John Wesley said at times about the Church of England. Although he remained a priest of that church he spoke and wrote at a time when a new community was in the process of being formed. A period such as this is always critical, for it is inevitably a time of serious polemic. Under such conditions restraint towards the parent community is indeed a sign of greatness and charity.

Against this background we may ask further whether the theological image of the Jews as expressed in the writings of St Chrysostom, the very fountainhead of mediaeval anti-Jewish prejudice, has any connection with certain statements and attitudes in the New Testament itself. For clarity and simplicity it may be permissible to reduce the image of the Jews in Chrysostom to two funda-mental assertions: first that Judaism is a decadent religion and second that the Jews are guilty of deicide. Everything else that St Chrysostom says can be viewed as an exten-sion of this caricature of Judaism, and one might even say that all the mediaeval denigration of the Jews is not much more than an embellishment of those two funda-mental accusations.

As soon as we inquire whether in the New Testament there is any such trace of caricature or fundamental accusation against the Jews we are not only faced with a host of New Testament problems but are also confronted with a vast literature on this and a great number of subsidiary questions. Try as we may, we can hardly answer our primary questions without being launched into such specialist questions as: What is the relation of Jesus to the Pharisees in the Synoptic Gospels? How do we explain the significance of 'the Jews' in St John's Gospel? What exactly was Jesus' attitude to the law and to the Jews as the Israel of God? Is St Paul's view the same as that of Jesus? How do the New Testament writers use the Old Testament and how are all these questions developed in the writings of the early Church Fathers? It may well be that such a formidable list is sufficient to disquiet us moderns, but we might at least receive some consolation from the fact that our nineteenth-century forebears would have written at least four volumes on what is here attempted in one chapter!

We may start our inquiry by questioning the Christian use of the term 'Pharisee'. Is it not true that this has become almost synonymous with the particular way in which the Pharisee is distinguished from the publican in the parable of Jesus in Luke 18? Claude Montefiore admits that

it cannot be doubted that this passage with its charming parable justly illustrates one of the dangers of Rabbinic legalism or if you will of the Rabbinic religion. Objections can only be raised when the parable is said to illustrate not the dangers and perversions of Rabbinic religion but the Rabbinic religion itself—as if the Pharisee of the parable was the average Pharisee and the average Rabbi produced by Rabbinic legalism, and worse still as if this odious Pharisee represented not the perversion, but the type and even the ideal—as if he is the very man whom the Rabbi would wish to be and was. I feel that this is false.[1]

In the different connotation in Montefiore's words 'cannot be doubted' and 'this is false' there is the difference between the condemnation of ostentation in prayer to which the Pharisees and most religious people are prone and the first step in a serious caricature of Judaism when this is applied as a blanket accusation not only to the Pharisees but also to their spiritual heir, Rabbinic Judaism. Yet is this not precisely what has happened? Not only is this the starting point but also practically the

[1] *Rabbinic Literature and Gospel Teachings* (Macmillan, London, 1930), pp. 368-9.

whole content of the Christian idea of the Pharisees. In fact the more we investigate the traditional Christian image of the Pharisees as it was applied in particular to the Jews, the more it becomes evident that this image rests on an immense caricature of what is said in the Gospels of certain trends among the first-century Pharisees, and has been mistakenly interpreted in the Christian tradition as a complete statement on Pharisaism and subsequent Judaism. If for example we consider the crucial New Testament passage on the Pharisees in Matthew 23, where Jesus speaks out against certain abuses in Pharisaic religion such as hearing and not doing, ostentatiousness in the practice of religion, making that practice burdensome, hypocrisy, legalism and externalism, are not these the very marks which we have so casually applied to the whole of Judaism?

By stressing that the New Testament picture of the Pharisees is not only one which picks out the points of failure but also one that is communicated to us at the points of controversy where Jesus and the Pharisees clash, be that over some aspect of the law such as sabbath observance, permissible grounds for divorce or the rights and wrongs of paying tribute to Caesar, this does not mean that we need to whitewash the Pharisees, for the history of Christianity has shown how prone all institutional religion is to the very weakness against which Jesus here pronounces.

All this is true and is today increasingly recognized by both Jews and Christians, but we need also to acknowledge that for a rounded picture of the Pharisees we must turn to their own literature. Our mistake has been that we have evaluated the Pharisees in terms of their failure and not also of their genuine achievements. There is genius as well as failure in Pharisaism and that genius is fully shown in the way in which the Pharisees applied the Torah to the minutiae of daily living and thus made it a religion that was firmly rooted in the common life of the Jewish people. Their vitality is vindicated in the very survival of Judaism and their piety shines forth clearly in the tenacity of Jewish martyrs to that form of religion to which they gave the main impetus. To give full recognition to this aspect of Pharisaic religion is in no sense glossing over their failure as described by Jesus. It is rather adjusting a Christian lopsidedness by allowing ourselves to face this form of religion fully. Not only must we determine the particular cast that the image of the Pharisees in the Gospel takes but, having recognized its particular partisan (not false!) purpose and approach, we need to fill up this picture by studies which describe the Pharisees from their own literature and against the background of their actual religious achievements—this and nothing less is what is involved in a 'Christian presence amid Judaism'.

This poses a problem. The more we acknowledge the achievements of Pharisaic religion the more it becomes necessary to ask why the conflict arose between them and Jesus. It is possible to maintain that such a conflict at that time was inevitable, for it was nothing less than a clash between two types of religion, one dynamic and the other institutional. This line of argument presupposes that Jesus was wholly outside the Pharisaic tradition. But are we not here reading back into the Gospel narrative the separation of Church from Synagogue of a later day? It seems far more in keeping with the Gospels to see Jesus as very much part of the Pharisaic tradition. Indeed, not only is it possible to find similarities between the teaching of Jesus and the Pharisees but even many of Jesus' strictures against the Pharisees can be paralleled in the rabbinic literature.

The actual conflict in the Gospels is highlighted in Jesus' attitude to the Law. We may take here, as the most crucial sayings of Jesus, 'Think not that I have come to destroy the Law or the Prophets; I am not come to destroy but to fulfil' and 'Ye have heard that it was said . . . but I say unto you . . . ' (Matt. 5.17, 21-22), and also the people's comment on Jesus' teaching, 'He taught them as one who had authority and not as the scribes' (Mark 1.22 and Matt. 7.29). It would be impertinent within the limited scope of this chapter to offer solutions of such notoriously difficult passages, the most we can hope for is to indicate a possible way of approach. The point of difficulty is centred in Jesus' affirmation 'to fulfil' with the apparent contradiction of his word of sharp contrast—'but I say'.

First, we need to take seriously the way in which the rabbinical gospel of Matthew illustrates Jesus' 'fulfilment' by way of extending the Law to its primal implications. So for instance, Jesus explains the prohibition of murder and adultery by extending the prohibition to the point where a wrong *attitude* to our neighbour or to a member of the opposite sex may eventually lead to the committing of murder or adultery (Matt. 5.21-28). Second, the form by which Jesus introduces this daring type of fulfilment 'but I say unto you' was not an unfamiliar phrase; rather it was the generally accepted formula for offering an original interpretation; but this sort of teaching was restricted to the fully accredited rabbi. The difference lies in a distinction between 'scribes and Pharisees'. The amazement of the people was that such a popular teacher as Jesus, who was much more easily classed with the 'scribes', should boldly use the most authoritative form reserved for the fully accredited rabbi.

The more usual explanation of how one might reconcile Jesus' two statements 'Not to destroy' and 'But I say' is to suggest that Jesus had a double attitude to the Law. Yet this is hardly satisfactory. It is far better to allow the rabbinical background to place in focus these two difficult sayings and to see them as not contradictory to each other but rather together defining Jesus' attitude to the Law as essentially 'constructive fulfilment'. Jesus does point out new meanings of the Law, not as one who destroys the Law but rather one who plumbs its inner meaning and so deepens its intention. In modern theological parlance we might dare to call it a 'fulfilment in depth'. It is not difficult to see how the more traditional explanation in terms of contrast tended to lead to the idea that Jesus abrogated the Law. Since the Law was so often taken and rightly seen as the very symbol of Judaism, this led all too easily to the idea that Jesus declared Judaism to be decadent.

Mention should also be made of a line of interpretation which suggests that the very placing of the new injunctions of Matthew 5 within the context of the Sermon on the Mount and the fact of Jesus' choice of twelve disciples and the use that Jesus made (in Matt. 21.31-46) of Isaiah's parable of the Vineyard and the cornerstone of Psalm 118, shows that Jesus was deliberately creating a 'New Torah' and a 'New Israel'. One cannot lightly set

51

aside this type of argument or exclude the idea of a 'New Torah' from the thought in the Sermon on the Mount, yet this need not necessarily be more radical than a new or novel interpretation of the Torah which uses a not altogether unknown concept in contemporary Judaism of that era. It is particularly evident in the Qumran movement. It would seem that a strict reading of Jesus' own words and actions do not amount to a 'New Torah' or a 'New Israel' in the sense that the 'Old Torah' was destroyed and that 'Old Israel' displaced. Certainly Jesus' use of such parables as the Vineyard did have undertones and warnings of rejection and displacement, but Jesus seems to be more in line with Isaiah's concept of the remnant that envisaged a new inner grouping within the community of Israel rather than the creation of a new community based on the total rejection of the old.

St John's Gospel has for long been considered the most anti-semitic of any writing in the New Testament, and this was deduced from the recurrent phrase 'the Jews' which appears some seventy times in the Gospel and plays such a significant role in the core of the Gospel's argument (chs. 5-12). In this Gospel 'the Jews' are portrayed not only as the opponents of Jesus but as 'in darkness' and 'blinded' so that they cannot even understand the implications of their own scriptures. This position was intensified by a generally accepted theory that this Gospel was essentially late and Hellenistic and that its purpose was to interpret Christianity in terms of current Greek philosophy essentially oriented to the non-Jewish world.

Recently this view has undergone a radical change. It has been pointed out that the whole orientation of the

Whose Bible?

Gospel is within the compass of the Jewish world. Even 'the side glances' to the Gentiles present in the other Gospels are missing. The only Gentile mentioned is Pilate. Jesus is seen as a direct extension of Moses, Abraham and Isaiah, and to these characteristically Jewish prototypes are added such striking Old Testament categories as 'the Manna', 'the Shepherd' and 'the Vine'. What does all this add up to? If the whole perspective of the Gospel is Jewish it could hardly have been directed to a non-Jewish world. Rather it is directed to the great number of Jews who as yet 'do not believe'. This does of course give an entirely new slant to the meaning of 'the Jews' in the Gospel. It can hardly be taken as a straightforward designation of the Jewish people. Just as in the Apocalypse we are accustomed to the need for interpreting the designation 'the Jews', so also in the Gospel we need to ask who really were meant by this title. Fortunately there are clues in the Gospel itself. It is a title quite obviously applied to 'the opposition', to those Jews who opposed and rejected Jesus. Some point out that it would be permissible in almost all instances to translate 'the Jews' as 'the Judeans' as in fact the RV Margin actually does in 7.1 and 11.7, 54. Others have suggested that it might be legitimate to translate for 'the Jews' sometimes 'the people' and at other times 'some of the people' or 'the assembly'. If once it was thought that this kind of translation was a way of toning down anti-Jewish tendencies in the Gospel, it can now be seen as a return to the original intention of the Gospel. If this line of argument in seeing the original meaning of 'the Jews' as referring to the opposing party within Jewry is right, then the conflict referred to in the Gospel is one essentially within the Jewish community. The situation is remarkably similar to that evident in Isaiah's prophecy, where harsh things are said about certain sections of the Jewish community—'sinful nation, a people laden with iniquity, a seed of evil doers, children that are corrupters' (Isa. 1.4). Such parallel accusations as there are in the Gospel are not a matter of theological prejudice imbued with racial overtones but rather a theological conflict within one community.

It is however true that such inner conflict as is reflected in the Gospel does very easily lead to separation; and, when the conflict here reflected is transposed to one between two mutually exclusive communities, what was originally said of the opposing party within one community is very easily said about the other community as a whole. What separates and distinguishes the one from the other is simply the time lag before the actual separation and usually the growth of one into a majority and the diminishing of the other into a minority. This is obviously what happened in the history of interpretation of 'the Jews' in the Fourth Gospel. The real issue for Christians today is to rectify any such wrong interpretations that have racial connotations and to face the implications of the original theological conflict here portrayed.

When we consider the relation of St Paul to the questions under review we need to remember that the views of the Apostle on these matters have often been misunderstood because it is not realized that however much Paul may have written on these issues they were still on the circumference of his teaching. At the centre of Paul's thought is his conviction that Christ is Lord, and from this formative belief everything else issues. This belief remains normative for all Christians of all time. At the turn of this century it was popular to believe that Paul had twisted the simple religion of Jesus into Christianity and that he did this mainly by welding it to Greek mystery religion. This and other factors gave rise to the 'bad Paul theory'. Since then, however, Paul has been exonerated and it is now generally agreed that he was much more of a Jew than a Greek. There would be few Jewish writers who today would deny the essential Rabbinism of Paul.

Where the question about Paul does arise is in his interpretation of the Law following upon his Christian experience. Paul's teaching on the Law is not easy to summarize. We might well begin with his statement that 'Christ is the end of the law' (Rom. 10.4). Here his meaning can be quite simply that Christ has brought into being a New Law, in line with the rabbinic belief that in the Messianic Age the Old Law is transcended by a new one. The above phrase may however not be as radical as this and may only mean that Jesus marks the end of the old *use* of the Law which function Paul goes on further to describe as being that of a 'schoolmaster to bring us unto Christ' (Gal. 3.24). From this pedagogic function Paul goes on to emphasize that the Law has always been impotent to engender right conduct, that he who fails to keep any one commandment fails to keep all the commandments, and that in this direction the Law not only serves to throw sin into open relief but also acts as a curse, as a force to death and not to life (cf. Rom. 3.19-20; 7.7; Gal. 3.10, 13).

Paul further reinforces his contention on the temporary nature of the Law and the fact that its main function

55

terminates with the event of Jesus by stressing that the trust relationship of Abraham was prior to the Law and is now supremely operative in the promises of God realized in Jesus Christ the Lord. And yet Paul adds as it were a postscript to his main treatise on the Law by almost going back upon what he has already said in asserting that the Law is permanent and good (Gal. 3.21; Rom. 7.12). This subtlety in Paul's teaching, so characteristic of him, is perhaps best explained as a genuine look over his shoulder at his co-religionists who do not admit the Messiahship of Jesus or share his thought on the Law.

Christian interpreters of the Apostle have tended to accept his summation of the Jewish teaching on the Law as measuring up to the fulness of the Torah. At this point even the most sympathetic Jewish interpreters of Paul have been obliged to take serious objection. In particular it has been argued (and argued well!) that in two significant directions Paul has violated the Jewish concept of Torah. First, he curtailed the meaning of Torah and, secondly, he developed new functions of the Law as he looked back upon its purpose from his experience of Jesus the Messiah.

It must at once be said in fairness to Paul and to all who share his experience that it is hardly surprising that such an all-important event as the recognition of Jesus as the Messiah should give him a new outlook on the central factor of his religion in his pre-Christian experience. Yet this justifiable looking back does not obviate the fact that in his looking back Paul did not do full justice to the rabbinic concept and use of the Law. Some would go even further and say that in much of what Paul says about the

Law he is hardly speaking the same language as the rabbis. It would appear that the Law in Paul's experience was a very different matter from the Torah in the experience of the rabbis as attested in their own literature. The rabbis might agree with Paul that not to keep the Law was a curse, but their understanding of this was crucially different from that of Paul. The curse for them would be in any reduction of the Law and not in the frustration of being made aware of the large and exacting demands of the Law that one was impotent to fulfil. Solutions are far from easy but perhaps a possible line of approach is given to us in the two most extreme sayings of the Apostle that 'Christ is the end of the law' (Rom. 10.4) and 'we establish the law' (Rom. 3.31). From this and other passages that we have quoted it is at least clear that Paul had a profound regard for the Torah; he did know something of its grandeur and strength, and perhaps that is why he could not indulge in a wholehearted denigration of the Law or totally renounce its practice. Yet Paul was also aware of the frustration and impotence that was possible in a religion of Torah. It would seem that the real clue to Paul's confused attitude to the Law arose out of a genuine religious crisis in which he could say 'the law is holy, and the commandments holy and just, and good' (Rom. 7.12), and at the same time triumphantly declare that he was 'delivered from the law', from the 'yoke of bondage (Rom. 7.6; Gal. 5.1). The rabbis and Paul are talking about the same thing but they are facing the Torah from opposite ends. Paul's dominant experience of the Law is at the point of its weakness and strain; the rabbis saw its aspect of strength and grandeur. It is easy to see how the Apostle, looking from this angle, did not do full justice to the rabbinic concept, but it is also true that the rabbis have not fully faced the weakness and strain in a religion of Torah and the challenge to reorient the Torah in new and demanding situations.

For both religions the attitude to Torah has once more become a contemporary crisis. A mere glance at an American Jewish periodical or Israeli newspaper would immediately illustrate this. For many Israeli Jews the demands of the Torah seem mere archaic intrusions making their life more difficult and uncomfortable. What can having milk in one's coffee after a meat course have to do with religion in the twentieth century? Or they question why mixed bathing should be associated with religious scruples in these days. Both are prohibited by the Torah! Similarly a flashback to some of the recent headlines in Church papers would indicate the utter chaos in contemporary Christian thought on the question of authority in moral values. It is a far cry from the revelation of a divine will in God's Law as the authoritative norm for Christian behaviour. But to return to our immediate theme, it is important for us to notice that if the Apostle was unfair to the totality of the Torah, then it is even more true to say that his interpreters ancient and modern have been far more unfair to him. The tendency was not only to develop one side of Paul's teaching on the Law but also to extend it and drive it to conclusions from which the Apostle himself shrank.

We turn now to consider particularly Paul's teaching on the composition of the Israel of God and to ask how this affected his views on the Jewish people and faith. This is classically expressed in Romans 9-11, though there are allusions elsewhere, particularly in Galatians.

Whose Bible?

The pivot of the Apostle's teaching rests on the differentiation between the empirical and the true Israel. He
points out that the extent of the true Israel has never
been determined simply on physical descent from Abraham, but rather on a spiritual affinity to Abraham's trust
relationship. He now sees the Israel of God as composed
of those Israelites who, true to their spiritual past, have
extended their trust relationship in dependence upon
Jesus as Lord, together with the Gentiles who have
entered into the covenantal relationship by their acceptance of Jesus. Yet this is not the whole truth for Paul.
He is embarrassed over the majority of Jews who are not
part of this Israel of God. This remains for the Apostle
the great concern and passion of his life, so that like
Moses he is willing to forgo his own personal salvation if
only 'Israel after the flesh' could be saved. Somehow he
cannot believe that the Jews as an ethnic unity, as a people
and religion, are totally and forever outside the Israel of
God. Almost in desperation he evolves his 'parenthesis
theory' and his elaborate imagery of the 'olive tree' and
of grafting and regrafting. In this way he is able to explain that what at that time appeared as a death blow to
Jewry, as their rejection, would yet turn out for their
final good and reinstatement. When this age of opportunity for the Gentiles had run its full and appointed
course then it would be consummated by the Jews in
their ethnic totality being reinstated in their proper place
in the Israel of God. No one can pretend (and Jewish
scholars do not!) that it is complimentary to the Jews to
be put 'on the shelf'. Yet, however convinced Paul may
have been that the rejection of Jesus by the majority of
his co-religionists was due to a 'hardening of heart' that

necessitated their momentary dispossession, on the question whether God had cast off his people he could only give one answer—'God forbid!' For Paul 'the gifts and calling of God are irrevocable' (Rom. 11.29).

So far we have dealt with some of the New Testament material that has some traces of anti-Jewish bias or—what is predominantly the case—that has been interpreted in an anti-Jewish direction and led to a caricature of Judaism and to the belief that in the Christian era it has become decadent. We need now to return to the other issue that we raised at the beginning of this chapter and to ask whether there is any New Testament evidence for the accusation that 'the Jews' were guilty of deicide. This is no straightforward issue but throws up a whole spate of interrelated questions. What were the real charges put up against Jesus? On what score and by whom was he actually condemned? What was the legal framework in which he was tried? How does the New Testament view the death of Jesus? Is the New Testament account of the passion biased against the Jews? For our present purpose we shall need to restrict ourselves to two questions. First, what is the basic New Testament account of the trial and death of Jesus and, secondly, does it represent the Jews fairly? From the outset we need to keep in mind that the New Testament gives a twofold reason for Jesus' death. On the one hand St Peter on the day of Pentecost is able to say quite directly 'Ye have taken and by wicked hands have crucified and slain' (Acts 2.23), and yet precedes this statement by the words 'Him being delivered by the determinate council and foreknowledge of God' thereby involving the will of God in the death of Jesus. The same double line of argument is true of St Paul. He like other

Whose Bible?

New Testament writers stresses the part played by our sin and the sin of all men in the death of Jesus. One can even see these twin concepts in the Gospels, 'the Son of man goeth as it was determined; but woe unto that man by whom he is betrayed!' (Luke 22.22). Christians have rightly interpreted this aspect of the death of Jesus in the credal statement 'who died for our sins' (I Cor. 15.3), but they also rightly include a personal name to remind us of the historical setting: 'was crucified under Pontius Pilate'.

When we turn to the trial of Jesus as recorded in the Gospels themselves the account in briefest outline sees a conflict between Jesus and the Jewish hierarchy reaching such dimensions that the latter decide he must be silenced. The occasion was Jesus' coming up to Jerusalem for the Passover feast and the opportunity was provided by a betrayal by one of his disciples. Jesus was accused before the Sanhedrin not only of claiming to be Messiah but also of claiming divine titles. This made him, in the eyes of the court, guilty of blasphemy which was punishable by death. Jesus was handed over to the Roman authorities, who did not seem to be convinced that he was politically dangerous enough to warrant swift removal; but because Pilate saw that Jesus was a figure of contention at a time when he could ill afford any kind of popular uprising, he gave way to the demands of the Jewish hierarchy and ordered Jesus to be scourged and crucified.

It would be surprising in the extreme if the Gospel narratives were lacking in some obscurity; indeed the more one compares the various accounts the more involved we see them to be so that the unravelling and piecing together of all the evidence has become a specialist's nightmare. Without entering into that nightmare, we may note that the most constant Jewish objection is that the Gospel narratives tend to exonerate the Romans and place the responsibility on the Jews. Yet the Gospels, it is agreed, do not omit any of the *dramatis personae* (be they for or against) in the passion story. Where there has been a serious shift of emphasis is in the way that Christians have interpreted the recorded events. More and more the trial and the crucifixion of Jesus were seen as something external to the Jewish people, something that the Jews inflicted on Christians. This is well borne out by the contemporary notions referred to at the beginning of this chapter. When Jewish scholars today emphasize the very real Roman involvement and stress that the Jewish role in all that happened at that time was essentially an internal issue they restore a perspective inherent in the Gospel narrative itself. Nothing could be further from the truth than that 'they' (the Jews) crucified 'our' (Christian) Jesus. In this strange kind of reading back the Jews have been saddled with an animosity against an outside group (i.e. the Christians) which finds its point of greatest calumny in their actually causing the death of 'our' leader; and, because of what Christians believe of Jesus, the Jews have been accused of deicide. It is at this point that we are most unfaithful to the Gospel story and it points to the evil of such a designation as 'the Jews' in this context. What of the Jews in the Gospel narrative who mourned for Jesus? What of the women of Jerusalem on the Via Dolorosa? What of the beloved disciple and of Mary the Mother of Jesus? What of Joseph of Arimathea? We have tended to think of these figures as Christians but they were no less Jewish than Judas Iscariot or members of the Sanhedrin. It is by rending the trial and death of Jesus from its setting and by losing the New Testament insight that the death of Jesus is God's way of annulling all Man's sin, including our own, that in our thinking we have transposed a terrible event in the Roman protectorate of first-century Judaea to an event which we now see as carried out by 'the Jews of all time' against the whole non-Jewish world in general and Christians in particular. It is this serious misrepresentation that Christians need to adjust.

So far, we have dealt with the obvious New Testament questions that relate to the earliest Christian attitude to the parent religion and people. Perhaps not so obvious an issue is the attitude of the New Testament writers to the Jewish scriptures of the Old Testament. But, as we shall see, in the way this question was developed in the period after the New Testament it is related to a serious spiritual disinheriting of the Jews that led directly to the idea that Judaism was decadent. However loaded this question of 'Whose Bible?' may have come to be after the New Testament period, it was at first quite natural that the New Testament writers should use the Old Testament as a scriptural authority to substantiate their messianic claims about Jesus. For us today, trying to discover exactly how the New Testament writers did use the Old Testament, there is first of all the rather complicated question as to what text of the Old Testament they used. Most of the textual differences between the New Testament quotations of the Old Testament and the accepted Hebrew text can be explained by the fact that the New Testament writers used the Septuagint; but this does not account for all the variations, much less for the conflation of the Old Testament texts such as is particularly evident in Matthew's Gospel.

Various theories of a very early Christian *Book of Testimonies* that predates our Gospels have been proposed, but these are not without their serious difficulties. It seems likely that there may well have been a very early Christian conflation of Old Testament texts that was available to our New Testament writers but this may have not been much more than a few 'fly-sheets'.

As to the actual use that our New Testament writers made of the Old Testament, it is clear that they both continued to use the scriptures in the ordinary Jewish way and at the same time developed their own radical interpretation. In this they were by no means the only innovators. The Qumran sect known to us from the Dead Sea scrolls also developed their own distinctive interpretation of the accepted Jewish scriptures but the Christians more than any other deviationists stressed the element of 'fulfilment' in their new interpretation. It is important, however, that we do not think of this fulfilment of the Old Testament as amounting to 'demonstrable proof' of the Christian position. The whole history of Christian-Jewish polemics shows how inconclusive such argument can be.

In an age when the idea of proving the existence of God was thought possible it was all too easy to note the idea of prediction and fulfilment in Matthew's Gospel and to interpret this in terms of proof. It was thought that the New Testament writers maintained that the Old Testament likenesses to actual incidents in the life of Jesus proved that he was the Christ, and that it was this clear proof from the Old Testament that engendered faith in the disciples. The truth is rather the reverse. Undoubtedly the disciples' understanding of the person and work of Jesus was enhanced by the suggestiveness of Old Testament passages associated with the Messiah; it is also true that Jesus himself does use Old Testament incidents and images by way of explaining his unique vocation. Yet in both cases the creative factor is the quality of Jesus' own person. The starting point is the sheer fact and event of Jesus.

Looking back upon the Old Testament from their experience of Jesus, the disciples could claim that they had both witnessed and experienced a true fulfilment of the Messianic expectation in the Old Testament. This fulfilment was for them not so much 'predictions coming off' but rather the conviction that the Christian interpretation of this or that Old Testament idea, statement or incident, was realized in Jesus the Messiah, was what the Old Testament was about. That at these points Christians differed from the way their fellow Jews would interpret the same Old Testament passages was hardly avoidable; it is after all the only way in which they could justify their differences from the majority of other Jews. This is however no reason, as we have seen, why at the same time Christians should not also continue to use much of the Old Testament in the same way as their fellow Jews and so in fact *share* the Old Testament scriptures with them. There is a great difference between the sharing of scriptures that is evident in the New Testament and subsequent Christian claims that only those who adhere to the Christian interpretation of the Old Testament understand any part of it, or can reasonably claim it as their own spiritual possession. Some might object here by

65

maintaining that there are times when the New Testament itself approaches very near to such an exclusive claim of the Old Testament. Is not this the contention of the Fourth Gospel (John 5.35) and the main argument of the Epistle to the Hebrews, which maintains that the central Old Testament figures and images were mere shadows of the realities actualized in Jesus? It is significant that in this instance the New Testament writers are in fact concerned to authenticate the Christian belief in Jesus and did not preclude a continuing Jewish interpretation of other aspects of the Old Testament of which the Fourth Gospel has many striking examples (cf. particularly John 10.34-35).

'There arose up a new king over Egypt, which knew not Joseph' is the laconic way in which the Book of Exodus introduces us to a far-reaching attack on Israel in ancient Egypt. It is unfortunately an equally appropriate introduction to the post-Apostolic development of these questions. The most forthright attack comes from Marcion, a Christian heretic and schismatic of the second century who pleaded for a total rejection of the Old Testament with its people and their God. He attempted to distinguish between the 'God and Father of our Lord Jesus Christ' and the God of the Jews in the Old Testament. His views were too extreme and too naively opposed to the Apostles' teachings for them to have had a chance of general acceptance. The Church realized that Marcion's teachings struck at the very roots and foundations of the Christian faith and so rejected them. While the flagrant anti-Jewish attitude of Marcion was rejected, a more subtle anti-Jewish attitude did find acceptance in the thought of the Church in the second century. This new attitude is epitomized in such second-century writings as the *Epistle of Barnabas* and Justin Martyr's *Dialogue with Trypho*. Not only were these writings crucial in determining the Church's attitude to the Jews in the post-Apostolic period, but the way in which the argument and scriptural expositions in them were reflected in subsequent so-called disputations with the Jews indicates that they were also normative in shaping what became the accepted attitude of the Church on the Jews and related issues.

Of the second-century writings Justin's *Dialogue*[1] is by far the most significant. Not only is it the largest (about the size of the four Gospels) and most comprehensive treatment of Christian-Jewish relationships in its time but also, despite its many harsh anti-Jewish statements, there still remain in it some faint traces of the Pauline conviction that 'God has not cast away his people' as evident in the somewhat grudging admission of Justin that 'your race shall not perish completely' (55.3). Another point in its favour is that one can still detect some genuine echoes of dialogue instead of the monotonous monologue of so many subsequent Christian-Jewish disputations. Although there are these and some other relieving features in the *Dialogue* it, together with the *Epistle of Barnabas* and other writings, indicates the increasing denigration of the Jews in this period.

From this it is not difficult to see how the two primary anti-Jewish accusations that we have noted in the writings of Chrysostom evolved. Whereas, for example in the New

[1] All quotations from the *Dialogue* are taken from Lukyn Williams' translation with introduction and notes (SPCK, London, 1930). See also by the same writer an outline work on Christian-Jewish disputations up to the Renaissance entitled *Adversus Judaeos* (Cambridge University Press, 1935).

Testament we see both Romans and Jews involved in the death of Jesus, the culpability is all too easily in Justin's *Dialogue* transferred wholly to the Jews. Even more regrettably, Justin suggests that the Jewish involvement in the death of Jesus is the cause of present Jewish suffering and misfortune:

that your lands should be desolate and your cities burned with fire, and that foreigners should eat up the fruits before your face, and none of you go up unto Jerusalem. . . . And therefore all this has happened to you rightly and well. For ye slew the Just One and His prophets before Him, and now ye reject . . . those that set their hope on Him (*Dial.* 16.2-4).

This and similar statements are relieved by a massive allegorization of the Old Testament that sees the cross foreshadowed in most unlikely Old Testament incidents. However forced and strange this may appear to us, it did in a measure preserve the New Testament insight that the death of Jesus was God's way of annulling man's sin. This theological aspect was, however, not strong enough to check an increasing concentration upon the Jew as the effective cause of the death of Jesus. It is but a small step from the contention of Justin that the sufferings of the Jews are related to their killing of Jesus, to that of justifying hatred and persecution of Jews because they are guilty of deicide.

Again, while in the New Testament there is a genuine sharing of the Old Testament with the Jews (admittedly this does not rule out the claim that God's saving acts in the Old Testament reached their intended culmination in Jesus), this is not sufficient for Barnabas. He is not content to share the Old Testament and its heritage with

Whose Bible?

the Jews but asserts that only Christians understood or indeed were ever intended to understand the scriptures:

... You see what an excellent lawgiver Moses was! Alas, how could those people grasp and understand these things? But we rightly understand and explain the commandments in the sense in which the Lord intended (*Ep. Barn.* 10.11-12).[1]

Justin makes a similar claim when he asserts:

They [Old Testament pointers to Jesus] are laid up in your scriptures, or rather not in yours but in ours, for we obey them but you, when you read, do not understand their sense (*Dial.* 29.2).

Very much the same applies to the precious Jewish conviction that they were the people of God. Justin finds no difficulty in boldly asserting that the Christians are

the true and spiritual Israelitish nation and the race of Judah and of Jacob and Isaac and Abraham (*Dial.* 11.5).

Barnabas places even more emphasis on this claim by suggesting that the Covenant never really did belong to the Jews:

... let us see whether the covenant which He had sworn to the fathers to give to their people was actually given. He has given it, but they, owing to their sins, proved unworthy of the favour.... Moses received it but they did not prove themselves worthy. But how did we receive it? Let me tell you. Moses received it as a servant, but the Lord in person gave it to us in order to make us the people of inheritance by suffering for our sake (*Ep. Barn.* 14.1-4).

[1] This and subsequent quotations from *The Didache, The Epistle of Barnabas*, etc., ed. and trans. by J. E. Kleist (Ancient Christian Writers 6), Longmans, London, 1948.

There is here a subtle but most significant shift of emphasis from the way in which the New Testament works out the composition of the Israel of God. While the New Testament may claim that the Church is the True Israel, it never extends that to mean that the Jews are totally excluded, or even worse, to the claim that they were never really included. There is a sense of mystery in the New Testament and particularly in the writings of Paul that are sadly missing in these post-Apostolic writings.

There is little need to go on emphasizing the growth of an anti-Jewish attitude in these writings. From a position in the New Testament where the great spiritual heritage of the Old Testament is shared with the Jews we see them in a few decades totally excluded from God's saving acts in the Old Testament. To this negative exclusion it was all too easy to add a positive assertion that claimed the blessings and heroes of the Old Testament as part of the Christian heritage and applied the curses and villains as belonging to the true history of the Jews.

To be fair, it must also be added that there was another side in the Christian attitude to the Jews epitomized by the phrase *Hebraica veritas*. This refers to a persistent though rather 'thin' Christian tradition of referring difficult points of Old Testament interpretation to the rabbis, thereby acknowledging their expert and worthwhile understanding of their own scriptures. In connection with the second-century writings that we have quoted, it is manifestly unjust to view these writings and their authors out of their time and the context of the Church's conflict with and separation from the Jews. The Church's polemic with the Marcionites and pagan Rome are also contributing factors. No doubt it is true that neither

Whose Bible?

Justin nor the writer of the *Epistle of Barnabas* purposely worked out an anti-Jewish policy; it was rather a by-product of their polemic on behalf of Christianity. Whatever may be the extenuating circumstances for these ancient Christian writers, there is no excuse for Christians today who have witnessed the tragic results of this anti-Judaic line of teaching not to rectify it in root and branch. It is such an intention that motivated an International Emergency Conference of Christians and Jews meeting after the holocaust of the second world war in 1947 at Seelisberg in Switzerland to issue ten significant points aimed at rectifying anti-Jewish elements in Christian teaching. It might well be opportune to turn them into a Litany of Christian Contrition.

THE TEN POINTS OF SEELISBERG

1. Remember that One God speaks to us all through the Old and New Testaments.

2. Remember that Jesus was born of a Jewish mother of the seed of David and the people of Israel, and that his everlasting love and forgiveness embrace his own people and the whole world.

3. Remember that the first disciples, the apostles, and the first martyrs were Jews.

4. Remember that the fundamental commandment of Christianity, to love God and one's neighbour, proclaimed already in the Old Testament and confirmed by Jesus, is binding upon both Christians and Jews in all human relationships without any exception.

5. Avoid disparaging biblical or post-biblical Judaism with the object of extolling Christianity.

6. Avoid using the word *Jews* in the exclusive sense of the enemies of Jesus, and the words *the enemies of Jesus* to designate the whole Jewish people.

7. Avoid presenting the Passion in such a way as to bring the odium of the killing of Jesus upon Jews alone. In fact, it was not all the Jews who demanded the death of Jesus. It is not the Jews alone who are responsible, for the Cross which saves us all reveals that it is for the sins of us all that Christ died.

   Remind all Christian parents and teachers of the grave responsibility which they assume, particularly when they present the Passion story in a crude manner. By so doing they run the risk of implanting an aversion in the conscience or sub-conscience of their children or hearers, intentionally or unintentionally. Psychologically speaking, in the case of simple minds, moved by a passionate love and compassion for the crucified Saviour, the horror which they feel quite naturally towards the persecutors of Jesus will easily be turned into an undiscriminating hatred of the Jews of all times, including those of our own day.

8. Avoid referring to the scriptural curses, or the cry of a raging mob: *His blood be upon us and upon our children*, without remembering that this cry should not count against the infinitely more weighty words of our Lord: *Father, forgive them, for they know not what they do*.

9. Avoid promoting the superstitious notion that the Jewish people is reprobate, accursed, reserved for a destiny of suffering.

Whose Bible?

10. Avoid speaking of the Jews as if the first members of the Church had not been Jews.[1]

[1] A leaflet including the Ten Points of Seelisberg can be obtained from the Council of Christians and Jews. General Secretary: the Rev. W. W. Simpson, 41 Cadogan Gardens, London SW3.

>>> >>>> <<<

3

The Question of Jesus

>>>◊<<<

If Jesus existed he existed as a Jew who lived and taught and died among his people; his people would be expected to remember him most clearly. Morris Goldstein

We Jews know Jesus in a way which is hidden from you Gentiles. Reported saying of Leo Baeck

THE first two chapters have been rather melancholy in tone. This is hardly avoidable when facing the nemesis of past Christian-Jewish relations, but it is an inevitable hurdle before we may hope for any new and valuable encounter. Even yet we are not through, for we now need to correct our misconceptions of what we have generally accepted as the Jewish reaction to Christianity in general and Jesus in particular. There is a deeply in-grained Christian conviction that 'the Jews' rejected Jesus coupled with the naive assumption that this was so from the very beginning. Quite simply, we must ask: Is this wholly true? Did 'the Jews' as such reject? We need only point to the Jewish origin of the Church and to the colossal upheaval at the entrance of the Gentiles into the Church to suggest that this conviction needs some quali-fication. If one can say, without defining the extent, that 'the Jews' rejected Jesus, then it is equally true to say

The Question of Jesus

that 'the Jews' accepted Jesus. However, both these statements are misleading. Yet they do stress that the issue
of Jesus has become and remains the loaded question *par
excellence* in the Christian-Jewish relationship. It is a
question that immediately recalls a long and intricate
history of reaction and counteraction. Despite all the
books that have been written by both Jews and Christians
on this subject, this question of Jesus has lost none of its
excitement; it remains a burning contemporary issue. So
we might instance the Biennial Conference of the Union
of American Hebrew Congregations, held in Chicago in
November 1963 when, suddenly and unexpectedly, Rabbi
Maurice Eisendrath in his presidential address raised the
question of Jesus. Commenting on the benefits that could
ensue from a genuine renovation of the Church's relationship to Jewry and Judaism the Rabbi dared to ask:

But what about our Jewish attitudes toward Christendom,
toward Jesus especially? Are we to remain adamant—orthodox—in our refusal to examine our own statements, our own
facts, our own interpretations of the significance of the life of
Jesus, the Jew? Have we examined our own books, official and
otherwise, to reappraise our oft-times jaundiced view of him
in whose name Christianity was established? How long can
we persist in ignoring his lofty and yet so simply stated prophetic and rabbinic teachings, merely on the grounds that he
repeated much that was voiced by his prophetic predecessors
and rabbinic contemporaries? Was Micah more spiritually and
morally original than Amos and Hosea? Do none of the rabbis
we revere and whose utterances we have our children master
repeat each other? How long shall we continue pompously to
aver that the chief contribution of Jesus was simply a rehash
of all that had been said before by his Jewish ancestors? How
long before we can admit that his influence was a beneficial

75

one—not only to the pagans but to the Jews of his time as well, and that only those who later took his name in vain profaned his teaching?

This statement brought forth a torrent of unfavourable Jewish criticism and one can only add that had such a statement been made in Israel, the reaction might well have been more adverse. In fact, something of the kind, though vastly different, did occur—it was nothing short of a furore in the Israel parliament, the Knesset. A heated debate centred around a Hebrew radio programme about Galilee, presented by Kol Yisrael, which had been written by Professor David Flusser, the Hebrew University's Jewish expert on the New Testament. The programme itself took the form of a descriptive journey through Galilee, which in passing mentioned some of Jesus' historical associations with that area. Religiously speaking it was completely innocuous, or so the directors of Kol Yisrael had supposed.

Rabbi Porush, a member of Knesset for the extreme religious party, raised the issue and requested that the programme be cancelled. He objected to new immigrants being subject to such subversive Christian propaganda. In a heated exchange with the Prime Minister he quoted the most severe Jewish scripture, 'thou shalt utterly detest it, and thou shalt utterly abhor it; for it is a cursed thing' (Deut. 7.26). (The use of this Deuteronomic text in a violently anti-Christian sense arose as a result of fierce Christian persecution in the mediaeval period.) Many varying views were expressed and not least a plea for charity and tolerance by the Prime Minister. What needs to be realized is that the whole range of the dispute was between Israeli Jews and that this portrays a great

The Question of Jesus

diversity of attitudes towards Jesus present in Israel today.

In the same year as this Knesset furore the present writer attended a lecture given by a visiting Christian professor on 'Jesus' attitude to the Law', which was part of the scheduled and advertised agenda of the Fourth World Congress of Jewish Studies held at the Hebrew University in Jerusalem in the summer of 1965. True, one could detect a certain undercurrent of strain during this lecture but the ensuing discussion remained scholarly and restrained. Further, there are Israeli Jewish publications which speak of Jesus as an integral and significant personage in the history of this land. By way of example we might quote from a recent work, *Daniel to Paul*, which devotes some thirty pages to an account of Jesus' life and teaching. On Jesus' 'personality and supreme religious authority' it says:

> Jesus is an outstanding example of the great prophets and teachers who emphasized the ethical and spiritual content of religion. Above all, it is impossible to separate his teaching from his life. He was one in whom life and teaching were one. Much of his teaching was original not so much in each individual idea but in relation to everything that he was and was trying to do. Jesus' impact on his deeply disturbed people and on succeeding generations cannot be decried. Even those who regard him from a purely human standpoint have done this aspect justice. Burning with prophetic zeal, dynamic, convincing, he could without apparent effort establish an immediate 'rapport' with his audience whether rustic or urban.[1]

[1] *Daniel to Paul*, ed. Gaalyahu Cornfeld (Macmillan, London [printed in Israel and there published by Hamikra Baolam, Tel Aviv], 1962), p. 259.

All this and much more that could be quoted in support (and by no means all as commendatory as the above) show how greatly the past determines the present in this on-going debate on Jesus and the Jewish people. Certainly there is here a very crucial issue for contemporary Jewry but let no Christian think that in *that past*, which so largely goes to make up the present ambivalent Jewish reaction to Jesus, Christians are faced with any less challenging issues. The average Christian perception usually starts with the Gospels and jumps directly to the contemporary situation; we need here to make good this gap —though it must be limited to the briefest outline.

The earliest extant Jewish reference to Jesus after the formation of the primitive Church is Gamaliel's 'sitting on the fence policy' recorded in Acts 5.39. 'For if this idea of theirs or its execution is of human origin, it will collapse; but if it is from God, you will never be able to put them down, and you risk finding yourselves at war with God.' This non-committal attitude, neither blaming nor praising, can be taken as epitomizing the Jewish reaction, almost up to the end of the first century. A great Christian scholar, Herbert Danby, steeped in the Jewish sources of this period, has summarized it most succinctly. He writes:

All the information we find in Jewish sources traceable to the first century shows that, in the beginning, the relations between the Jew and the Jewish-Christians were amicable; and what is far greater matter for surprise the Jewish attitude to our Lord Himself is, the earlier we penetrate, marked by the less degree of hostility. We are forced to the conclusion that so long as Pharisaic Judaism . . . records personal or almost personal reminiscences of our Lord, the surviving

78

record is not viciously hostile (as later became the case).[1]

There is an obvious divergence between this attitude to Jesus and his Church and what Christians have always imagined the Jewish attitude to be. What is even more perplexing is that Christians, by the end of the first century, in the writings of Barnabas and later Justin, treat Jews as hostile outsiders and the Jewish attitude in contemporaneous sources echoes this hostility, so very different from the attitude described above. The truth is, that the period of separation which provides us with clues to the understanding of this antipathy, was both longer and more intricate than Christians have generally recognized. It spans the period from the time when those Jews who accepted Jesus were allowed to remain within the Jewish fold up to the time when their Jewishness was denied them and thereafter it was only possible for individual Jews to withdraw from the Jewish community and join a predominantly Gentile Church. Most scholars now acknowledge that the period of separation was a crucial time for both religions. This was certainly the case for Christianity, but it might be argued that for Judaism it was nothing more than the expulsion of a minority deviationist group. It so happens that it was also the formative period when Judaism had to adjust itself to the loss of its central place of worship, the Temple, and of the sovereignty of its people in their national homeland. This readjustment can mainly be seen in the production of the Talmud which so admirably answered to the spiritual and cultural needs of the Jews in the Diaspora.

[1] H. Danby, *The Jew and Christianity* (Sheldon Press, London, 1927), pp. 8-9.

The crucial period of separation spans the time from the commencement of the first Jewish revolt in 66 to the collapse of the second revolt under Bar-Kochba in 135. These all-important seventy years in the relation of Jews and Christians are by no means a simple story; they form a complex pattern of historical events shot through with theological controversy that very largely determined the reaction of withdrawal and separation of the Church from the Synagogue that William Temple so rightly called the first schism in the People of God.

The theological controversy that lies behind the several acts of withdrawal by Christians and expulsion by Jews could be summarized as the ethnic implications of Torah over against the universalistic impetus of Christianity. In other words is was a question of fidelity to the Law with its involvement of national loyalty to the Jewish people over against the Christian conviction that the acknowledgement of Jesus as the Messiah called forth a loyalty and mission that reached out beyond the confines of Torah and nation. The issue is further complicated by the fact that this was both a tension between Jews and Christians and also between conflicting parties within the primitive Church itself. Most Christians are familiar with this conflict from the New Testament and in particular from Galatians and Acts 11 and 15, but this merely reflected the far more serious tensions between the Church and its parent community that reached a crisis in the outbreak of the first Jewish revolt. The Church of Jerusalem at the time was faced with the challenge of identifying itself with the revolt or declaring by its very refusal to throw in its lot with its fellow Jews that belief in Jesus as the Christ transcended such loyalties. The answer that the Jewish-Christian community in Jerusalem gave was somewhat indefinite. The majority felt keenly the tension of divided loyalties and so attempted to avoid the issue by withdrawing from Jerusalem.[1] It was not, however, a total withdrawal, for even a list of Jewish-Christian bishops of Jerusalem available to us from the fourth-century Christian historian Eusebius postdates the fall of Jerusalem in 70 and terminates with the collapse of the second revolt in 135.

The destruction of the Temple at this time did much to convince Christians that Jewry had been judged and brought to an end, but even this did not effect a total withdrawal from the parent community. Evidently not a few Christians clung to their membership in the other surviving and now dominant Jewish institution—the Synagogue. But by this time the very action of a large-scale Christian flight from Jerusalem at a time of Jewish crisis, the interpretation that many Christians gave to the destruction of the Temple and the extension of St Paul's concept of 'the end of the law' brought about a negative reaction from the Jewish leaders of the time. Evidently the rabbis became convinced that the Christians were endangering the very ethos of Judaism. For the rabbis, it must be remembered, the Torah was and remains God's unchangeable expression of his will for Israel. It was the indispensable framework within which the covenantal relationship between God and his people was experienced. Entrance into and participation in God's covenant could not be separated from the Torah, and so the rabbis could not conceive any differentiation within the totality of the Torah. All this the Christians challenged

[1] Cf. Eusebius, *Ecclesiastical History* III.5.3.

81

both by their teaching and practice, as was evident in the open way in which they received Gentiles into membership. It thus became clear to the rabbis that they could no longer view the Christian messianic sect with indulgence, for they realized that they were not merely dealing with a minority group that deviated on such a peripheral issue as the messianic allegiance to Jesus at first seemed to be. So, in keeping with their principles on the essential nature of Torah and its unique link with the Jewish people, around the year 90 they initiated some very definite measures which were aimed at detecting Christians in the Synagogue and as far as possible excluding them from its fellowship. The particular method that the rabbis adopted for effecting this expulsion of Christians from the Synagogue was the addition of a malediction against heretics in general and Christians in particular to a statutory part of the daily Synagogue service known as the Eighteen Benedictions.

Even this drastic action was not completely successful for we find that in the second Jewish revolt led by Bar-Kochba from 132 to 135 it was not yet taken for granted that Jewish Christians would not take part. The final blow came when Rabbi Akiba, the undoubted religious leader, with the tremendous prestige of standing in the line of Hillel, acclaimed Bar-Kochba as Messiah. This was the death blow to Jewish-Christian hopes that their fellow Jews might yet acknowledge Jesus as Messiah and the closing of the door upon what had remained until then in some sense an open question. Whatever uncertainty might until this event have lingered in the Christian community as to whether Jewish Christians should join the Jewish revolt against pagan Rome was now dispelled.

The Question of Jesus

There could be no compromise on the Messiahship of Jesus. If it was a question of Bar-Kochba or Jesus, quite obviously a Christian had no choice. While a Jew could still join the revolt and yet not accept Bar-Kochba's Messiahship, such a possibility was no longer open to a Christian, however much he cherished his place in the community of his people.

Perhaps no other events than those described above in the long history of the Jewish-Christian relationship illustrate so pointedly the theological tensions between the two religions. One can see the arguments for and against on both sides, and undoubtedly in this vital controversy mistakes were made by each disputant. It seems that the whole issue was faced with an 'either . . . or' attitude rather than one of 'both . . . and'. Is it possible that both insights may be necessary for a religion of world-wide scope and competence? Can they not have a refining and complementary effect on religion as they are allowed to interact, the one upon the other?

This much one can say when viewing the controversy from the twentieth century, but the truth is that subsequent evaluation, both Christian and Jewish, has gone beyond the evidence. It is generally supposed that Judaism in the Christian era gave up its universalistic aspiration, but that is as misleading as the sentiment that ever since this early conflict Christianity has thrown over every aspect of Law. Just as Christians can point to that part of their tradition that is in line with Jesus' great affirmation of the Law in Matt. 5.17, so likewise can Jews point to that continuing aspect of their teaching and practice regarding proselytes and the universalistic aspirations of Judaism.

We shall not be far from the truth if we acknowledge that both religions possessed some estimate of Law and some universalistic outreach, but that the first was only absolutely adhered to in Judaism and the second only wholeheartedly exploited in Christianity. This may be an evaluation that Jews and Christians are able to make today as they look back on the fierce controversy of the past, but it is surely too much to expect from the combatants at the time. To Judaism it seemed that what happened showed beyond all doubt that the Christian deviationist movement had taken a very definite non-Jewish turn and could no longer remain within the Jewish fold. Its future at this time did not greatly concern the Jewish leaders. As for the Christian Church, the strife we have just described not only confirmed it in a predominantly Gentile role but also marked the virtual death of Jewish Christianity. Unfortunately, the few Jews who subsequently joined the ranks of the Church were under continual pressure to despise and reject their Jewish heritage and to view their new-found membership as altogether contradictory to their former allegiance. In such a climate the few Jewish converts all too often reacted violently against their past and became the vanguard of the proponents of anti-Jewish attitudes. As the primitive Jewish-Christian element dwindled, the emergent Catholic Church took up an increasingly antagonistic attitude to the parent religion and that not surprisingly had its counterpart reaction among Jews.

It should not now surprise us that in subsequent Jewish sources there is but little trace of the Jewish reaction to the Christian movement and its founder. The first Jewish source available to us is Josephus, who is, as it were, on the boundary of this period of separation and whose writings form a useful bridge to the normative Jewish writings of the Talmud. Josephus has only one direct reference to Jesus and that is in his *Jewish Antiquities*. Although the trustworthiness of Josephus' testimony to Jesus has often been called into question, the few crucial lines that describe Jesus as 'a wise man, a doer of wonderful works and a teacher of such men as receive the truth with pleasure'[1] are now recognized to be genuine by both Jewish and Christian scholars. The very brevity of this reference conveys the Pharisaic attitude of not wishing to say too much and yet almost echoing Jesus' popular acclamation recorded in the Gospels: 'He is a good man' (John 7.12).

Christians have long been intrigued by what the most characteristic and authoritative Jewish writing known as the Talmud has to say about Jesus. Unfortunately, in the Middle Ages Christians were so ignorant of the contents of the Talmud that they were all too easily taken in by so-called Christian experts, regrettably often converted Jews, who maintained that the Talmud was full of animosity to Jesus. This resulted in a very negative attitude to the Talmud, which, at best, was spurned and at worst, confiscated, expurgated or even totally destroyed. The first Christian scholar to challenge this absurd notion that the Talmud was full of anti-Christian sayings was John Reuchlin in the sixteenth century. The real truth was almost the opposite of what had been accepted by Christians, for any objective inquiry into the extant references to Jesus and Christianity in the Talmud exposes the extreme paucity of the evidence. So much has this been

[1] *Antiquities* XVIII.3.3.

the case, that scholars have often spoken of the 'silence of the Talmud on Jesus'.

This need not surprise us in view of all that preceded the Talmud's composition. Christianity was now pursuing its non-Jewish path, and as far as the rabbis were concerned was no longer of any great interest to them. What is so often forgotten is the simple and compelling fact that the originators of the Talmud were greatly preoccupied with their own contemporary religious problems. They faced the challenging task of making Judaism relevant in the new conditions of the loss of national independence which was for them a far greater challenge than the rise of Christianity.

In any attempt to assess the Jewish reaction to Christianity in these normative Hebrew sources we have to pay extreme attention to the composite nature of the Talmud. The earliest and most authoritative portion of the Talmud is the Mishna, about twice as large as the New Testament. The writers of the Mishna are known as the Tannaim and correspondingly the period of their writing is termed Tannaitic. Following on the work of the Tannaim are the Amoraim who are largely responsible for the two commentaries on the Mishna known as Gemara. Each Gemara, together with the Mishna is called a Talmud. The Jerusalem or Palestinian Talmud, which took its origin in the Holy land, was completed at the beginning of the sixth century and the other, the Babylonian Talmud, which emanated from the Jewish schools in Persia, was completed towards the end of the same century.

All the extant references to Jesus in the Tannaitic tradition of the Talmud do not give us much information.

The Question of Jesus

All that we can say with certainty is that Jesus was remembered as a notable teacher whose disciples (strangely enough only five) carried on his teaching and healing ministry. Although his teaching is considered sufficiently heretical to be the cause of his death, the fact that he continued some of the Pharisaic teaching tradition is not forgotten. What is, however, of far greater significance than these meagre details, is the consistent agreement of all the evidence that Jesus remained a Jew. It was as such that he was valued and as such that his place in 'the world to come' was not denied. More than this we cannot say.

Nothing of startling significance was added during the second formative period of the Talmud's evolution, i.e. the time of the Amoraim from the third to the fifth century. There is a decreasing knowledge of Jesus, so that distinguished rabbis can even confuse his identity in the Talmud and mistake the time of his birth by more than a hundred years. All that we can deduce with confidence is that Jesus is still considered as being well-disposed toward his people Israel and that even in this later era Jesus has not been excluded from the commonwealth of Israel. In fairness to the evidence we must add that the earlier tradition that Jesus' teaching was heretical or, in the words of the Tannaim, that his teaching 'led Israel astray' is now intensified.

There is however a more indirect reaction at this later stage of which there is only a very faint trace in the Tannaitic tradition. We find a growing emphasis upon the unity of God, that allows for no plurality, upon the immanence of God, that needs no incarnation, upon the inviolability and permanence of the whole Law, that allows for no limitation of any kind, upon the superiority of the Law's own inherent authority, that makes confirmation by miracles unnecessary and upon Israel's Messianic hope in the future, that proves that the Messiah has not yet come. All this can easily be demonstrated from the Talmud but there is nothing new about it! We are not here confronted with the evolution of new doctrines but merely the strengthening of existing Jewish beliefs that are implicit (and to some extent already explicit) in the Judaism of Jesus' time. What is perhaps the most arresting feature of the Talmudic evidence is the way in which a differential is maintained between the person of Jesus and his teaching. Whereas less and less may actually be known about Jesus he is always remembered as a Jew. Almost the opposite is true of his teaching. At first, apparently, acceptable points were remembered but increasingly as Jesus' teaching is equated with Christian doctrine it is condemned entirely as altogether misleading, something to be resisted and rejected and against which Jewish beliefs, as we have noted above, need to be reinforced.

It is not a straightforward progression to pass from this restrained evaluation of Jesus in the Talmud to the phantasies of the Middle Ages. As we proceed to assess a rather notorious mediaeval Jewish 'Life of Jesus' we need to remind ourselves continually of the unpleasant truths of the Christian attitude and treatment of the Jews, which we attempted to face earlier. This is the real background to such a document as the *Toldot Yeshu*. In view of what was happening at that time it is no wonder that there is a world of difference between what was recorded of Jesus in the Talmud and the unattractive details of *Toldot Yeshu*.

This strange life of Jesus has many textual oddities and

one cannot be more definite about its dating than to place it sometime between the sixth and tenth centuries. It is so obviously a deliberate parody that it seems beside the point to discuss it as though it were intended to be taken for straightforward historical prose. But read apart from its historical context, it is an appalling and degrading account of Jesus and as such, beyond defence. When, in fact, we see it for what it is, the product of a defence mechanism against Christian persecution and continual pressure to convert, we might well be surprised that it is not much worse. The Jews at this time were continuously subjected to Christian propaganda, inflating the superiority of Christian doctrine, and hence there arose this refutation of Christianity in Jewish folklore. Great emphasis is placed on Jesus' illegitimate birth, and the source of his supernatural powers is traced to an unscrupulous acquisition and deployment of the secret letters of the Ineffable Name. In an age that was permeated with ideas of the supernatural this kind of parody was the only effective weapon against the persistent vindication of Christian truth in terms of the miraculous. Modern readers, both Jews and Christians, are appalled by such writings but the real evil persists when such works as the *Toldot Yeshu* are quoted out of context so that the underlying irritants are not exposed. Besides all this, it is worthwhile to reflect that neither Jesus' Jewish origin nor his outstanding success as a Jewish teacher and worker of miracles are denied, though they are certainly perverted. Seen from this angle, the *Toldot Yeshu* is an oblique confirmation of the Tannaitic tradition that at no single point excludes Jesus from Jewish traditions or denies his unusual role.

It cannot however be denied that *Toldot Yeshu* and similar degrading stories about Jesus have had an evil effect that has penetrated deep into the Jewish image of Jesus. Even today in Israel the present writer has heard the title of *Yeshu* used as a designation of Jesus in a derogatory sense (for this reason Christians have always preferred *Yeshua*, meaning salvation, as the proper Hebrew designation for Jesus) that indicates an association with the incidents recorded in *Toldot Yeshu*. This lays a responsibility on Jews to eradicate this wholly fictitious and unworthy representation of Jesus.

Toldot Yeshu is fortunately not the only mediaeval document from which we may deduce the Jewish attitude to Jesus and Christianity at that time. Despite the drawback of many weary disputations which were forced upon the Jews and which to a very large extent merely reflect what Christians at that time thought the Jewish answer to Christianity should be, there are also some Jewish works that give us new and valuable information. Firstly, there is what may perhaps be the only positive result of the forced disputations, a great increase in the actual Jewish acquaintance with the facts and sources of Christianity. This stands in sharp contrast to the meagre knowledge evident in the Talmudic era. Secondly, there are some serious and detailed Jewish criticisms of Christian doctrine, in particular the Trinity, and of the normative source, the New Testament. Thirdly, there is a surprisingly liberal addition in a recognition by some significant Jewish writers that Christianity has a positive value in that it has spread a diluted form of Judaism throughout the Gentile world. Maimonides, the outstanding twelfth-century philosopher, spokesman and exegete of mediaeval Judaism, extended this positive appreciation of Christianity by admitting that Christianity helped indirectly to hasten the coming Messianic Age because it transmitted to the world at large a partial knowledge of Torah.

All this may not seem a very great advance, viewed from the Christian point of view, but it is at least a first step toward the unusual position worked out by a most distinguished early twentieth-century Jewish philosopher Franz Rosenzweig. In an entirely new kind of disputation, in letters sent between the trenches in the first world war, Rosenzweig and his Christian counterpart, Eugene Rosenstock-Huessy, wrestled with the idea that there is a distinctive value of Jesus the Jew for the Gentile world that the Jews can recognize, without giving up their distinctive religion developed and maintained apart from Jesus. That is true, for the past and the present, but in this remarkable Jewish-Christian encounter both disputants attempted to reach out to each other at a deeper level. They recognized that for the present their discovery of each other was hidden in history, yet they entertained the hope that somewhere and somehow in the future there will be a true meeting, a unity that will do away with the agony of the historic separation.

Before leaving the mediaeval era we need to note in passing that, naturally enough, Christians have supposed that of far greater significance than the individual variations of the Jewish attitude to Christianity are the deviationist groups and movements. Jewish mysticism was the movement, *par excellence*, where Christians expected to find some outreach to Christian concepts, away from the hard realism of the rabbis. If we are to maintain

91

a right perspective, we need to be wary of such expectations, where so often wishful thinking is substituted for genuine evidence. Generally, it is not a matter of deliberate dishonesty but rather of a confusion of terms and ideas. What may at times legitimately be described as an approximation to Christian doctrine is too often interpreted as an outreach or longing after Christian truth. Approximation may be due to parallel movements or a common origin on which both Judaism and Christianity are dependent, whereas outreach and longing suggest that from a position of inner deficiency there is a gravitation to another and more satisfying position.

With this warning in mind we may note that Christian scholars often suspected that in the mythological and esoteric oddities of the Kabbala there might well be not only a reaction fundamentally different from that of the rabbis but also a serious rebellion against the austere rabbinical concept of God's unity. There was much to tempt Christian scholars to see in the complicated symbols and ideas of divine emanations, so prevalent in mediaeval Jewish mysticism, known as Kabbalism, a definite outreach toward Trinitarian belief. A more natural explanation is to interpret the Kabbalistic concept and approach to God as an approximation to Christianity on account of their common participation in mysticism, rather than as an outreach to a particular aspect of the Christian belief in God—the Trinity, a belief which Christian mystics found most truly attractive and satisfying. It is due to the authoritative work of Professor Gershom Scholem[1] that the complex origin of Jewish and Christian mysticism

[1] *Major Trends in Jewish Mysticism*, Thames and Hudson, London, 1955.

and their common indebtedness to gnosticism is now widely recognized. We cannot condemn the former line of Christian interpretation too harshly, for it seems that the Christian suspicion that there was something essentially non-Jewish about the mystical approach and its concept of God was, until Gershom Scholem, also upheld by the majority of Jewish scholars, whose antagonism was further reinforced by the actual conflict between some of the noted guardians of rabbinism and some of the leading exponents of mediaeval Kabbalism. Very much the same is true for a parallel eighteenth-century Jewish movement, Hasidism, that to mysticism added a specific ecstatic element not altogether unlike Protestant Pentecostalism.

Jewish modern history begins in the eighteenth century, in a new era when Europe was changing almost as much as Africa is today. These changes affected the Jewish community in every area of its life, and not least in its relationship to Jesus and Christianity. For our present purpose it is sufficient to trace this reorientation into diametrically opposed movements that can each be described in a single word: the first, assimilationism and the second, Zionism. The sudden crumbling of the ghetto walls not only opened the doors to western culture but also seemed to incite the liberated Jew to identify himself with his new environment to an extent where his identity as a Jew became dangerously blurred. For some, this process of assimilation did not even stop there. Western culture was so inextricably intertwined with Christianity that in many instances the first tide of emancipation and assimilation swept Jews irresistibly to the baptismal font. It looked dangerously possible that the most novel Jewish response to Christianity might well be utter capitulation and complete identification with the culture and religion of the Gentile majority. It was the determination to beat back the tide of such capitulation, which could only lead to Jewish disintegration, that in the eighteenth century to a great extent inspired the modern architect of Jewish emancipation, Moses Mendelssohn, to work toward the establishment of a reformed Judaism that should be concerned with eternal truths and freed from the mantle of a bygone past.

It is beyond our purpose to present an analysis of liberal or reformed Judaism, but there can be little doubt that its prime motivation was to readjust Judaism to the needs of the modern Jew. That this adjustment was carried out under the pressure of a society that was closely identified with Christianity is a mere accident of history, but the fact that this new Judaism aimed at equipping Jews to live *alongside* and no longer *separate* from their Christian neighbours involved a new orientation to Christianity in general and to Jesus in particular.

Another novel factor was a somewhat delayed reaction to emancipation. This ran altogether counter to the assimilationist policy, which accepted the European national structure as an essential framework for Jewry, and began to reassert Jewish nationalism: Zion and Zion alone was to be the true setting for the Jewish people. Zionism accepted the fact that there was a fundamental difference between the Jewish people and other nations, but maintained that the distinctive Jewish ethos and values could only be sustained in the same manner as the distinctiveness of other nations. Boundaries there must be, but not those of ghettos or of eternal truths; the only adequate ones were those of an independent sovereign state. It goes without saying that this new national awareness had its own response to a Christianity that appeared to be the one common denominator in the other nations, who had reduced the Jewish people to a shameful ghetto existence and would be unlikely to impose less humiliating conditions in a so-called emancipated era.

If, however, we select a representative group of Jewish writers it would not be possible to determine their attitude to Jesus on the simple score of whether they are pro- or anti-Zionist, since many other factors are involved in determining the modern Jewish evaluation of Jesus. Heinrich Graetz (1817-1891), quite apart from any novel ideas he held about Jesus, is particularly important in any modern appraisal of the Jewish attitude, on account of the enormous influence of his great work, *The History of the Jews*. This was the staple diet of practically every middle-class Jewish home of the last century. Graetz' evaluation of Jesus comes almost as a thunderbolt from the clear sky of a particularly restricted orthodox Judaism. Kabbalism and Hasidism are denounced as altogether non-Jewish; the references to Jesus in the Talmud and particularly the subsequent folklore of *Toldot Yeshu* are rejected out of hand, but Jesus himself is reclaimed as a great seer. Graetz writes:

The birthplace of Jesus, Nazareth, offered no particular attraction. . . . His small stock of learning and his corrupt half-Aramaic language pointed unmistakably to his birthplace in Galilee. His deficiency in knowledge, however, was fully compensated by his intensely sympathetic character. High-minded earnestness and spotless moral purity were his undeniable attributes; they stand out in all the authentic

95

accounts that have reached us, and appear even in those garbled teachings which his followers placed in his mouth. The gentle disposition and humility of Jesus reminded one of Hillel. . . . Like Hillel, Jesus looked upon the promotion of peace and the forgiveness of injuries as the highest form of virtue. His whole being was permeated by that deeper religion which consecrates to God not only the hour of prayer, a day of penitence, and longer or shorter periods of devotional exercise but every step in the journey of life, which turns every aspiration of the soul towards Him, subjects everything to His will, and with child-like trust, commits everything to His keeping.[1]

The nobility of this estimate needs no further comment, but the extent to which it was original is difficult to determine as similar ideas were being expressed by others at that time. Perhaps the most striking feature of Graetz' account is that his generous estimate of Jesus is also extended to his teaching and to the early Christian Jewish community. Graetz finds it possible to say that 'Jesus made no attack upon Judaism' (p. 155). He is even ready to admit that Jesus extended Judaism. 'The merit of Jesus,' he says, 'consisted principally in his efforts to impart greater force to the precepts of Judaism, in the enthusiasm with which he followed them out himself, in his ardour to make the Judaeans turn to God' (p. 156). In writing of the earliest disciples Graetz comments, 'His disciples who had remained true to Judaism promulgated the declaration of their master—"I am not come to destroy, but to fulfil; till heaven and earth pass, one jot or one tittle shall in no wise pass from the Law till all be

[1] *The History of the Jews*, Eng. trans. by Bella Loewy (5 vols., David Nutt, London, 1891), vol. 2, pp. 149-50.

The Question of Jesus

fulfilled" (Matt. 5.17)' (p. 155). He adds further that 'His disciples were hourly expecting the return of Jesus, and in this respect only differed from the Judaeans in so far as they thought the Messiah had already appeared in human form and character' (p. 168). On the death of Jesus Graetz writes, 'He is the only mortal of whom one can say without exaggeration that his death was more effective than his life. Golgotha, the place of skulls, became to the civilized world a new Sinai' (p. 166).

We can feel the drop in temperature when Graetz describes the activities of St Paul. He is seen as one who

endeavoured to destroy the bonds which connected the teachings of Christ with those of Judaism. . . . Paul not only disapproved of the so-called ceremonial laws of Judaism, but also of those relating to morality. He affirmed that without the law men would not have given way to their evil desires (p. 231).

For Graetz, Paulinism is the obvious missing link between an early Judaic Christianity and the contemporary Gentile face of Christianity, which for him is demonstrably contrary and opposed to Judaism.

It would seem that the only criterion for this and almost all Jewish commendation of Jesus' teaching was its similarity and indebtedness to rabbinism, but on any showing this is a very limited appraisal of both the content and effectiveness of that teaching for which Christian scholars have found no other adequate adjective than unique.

All generalizations have their exceptions, and so has the above. Claude Montefiore, the renowned liberal Jewish scholar of the early twentieth century, was particularly concerned with this partial and restricted view of the teaching of Jesus. He seems to detect this particular weakness when he points out that

. . . the originality and the greatness of the teaching do not depend so much on the details of the particular things said as upon the manner in which they are said and still more upon their effect as a whole. To each individual striking utterance of Jesus it is likely enough that a good parallel can be found in the rabbinic literature, but when Jewish scholars adopt this method of disproving the originality of the Gospel, they forget (quite apart from questions of date) the size of the Talmud and the Midrashim. The teaching of Jesus is contained in three little books which do not fill more than sixty-eight double-column pages of tolerably small print. The teaching belongs or is attributed to one man, and constitutes, in large measure a consistent and harmonious whole. It is not a combination of a thousand different occasional and disconnected sayings of a hundred different rabbis.[1]

This, it must be admitted, is an extremely liberal point of view, which in the person of Claude Montefiore was accompanied by the acceptance of Judaism as a western religious denomination, capable of maintaining its life in a predominantly non-Jewish environment.

Very different was the attitude of Asher Ginsberg (1856-1927), popularly known by his pen-name as Ahad Ha-Am (One of the People). His views were in direct contradiction not only to those of Claude Montefiore but also to any kind of assimilationist thought. This need hardly surprise us in the poet of Zionism, who propounds a distinctive Jewish teaching free from any non-Jewish

[1] *Some Elements of the Religious Teaching of Jesus* (Macmillan, London, 1910), p. 110.

98

traits and liberated from the context of a foreign environment.

In the prolific writings of Ahad Ha-Am one is hard pressed to trace any reference to Christianity. In one article published in 1910 in an extremely influential Hebrew periodical, originated and edited by Ahad Ha-Am, he expresses his views on 'Judaism and the Gospels'.[1] There is no single word of praise either for Jesus or the Gospels. Even specific mention of Jesus is avoided as far as possible in preference for the more impersonal designation of the New Testament or the Gospels. Commenting on Montefiore's work on *The Synoptic Gospels* he agrees that a Jewish evaluation is needed, but only for the specific reason that Christianity might be seen for what it is and its effects upon the Jewish minority clearly separated from the general pressures of a non-Jewish environment. For him a Jewish appreciation of the Gospels is so demonstrably alien to the essential character of Judaism as to make one fact clear beyond any shadow of a doubt to any Jew to whom Judaism is still alive: 'that the Gospels can be received only into a Judaism which has lost its own true spirit and remains a mere corpse.'

Ahad Ha-Am seems to be convinced that a true Jewish study of the Gospels can yield only one conclusion: that there exists an immense gulf between Judaism and Christianity, which he sees as an essential incompatibility between the Jewish preference for 'abstract ideal' and the Christian fondness for 'human likeness'. He writes:

[1] This article together with other essays was translated into English by Leon Simon and published under the title *Essays on Zionism and Judaism* (Routledge, London, 1922). Quotations from pp. 228-9.

The essential characteristic of Judaism which distinguishes it from other religions is its absolute determination to make the religious and moral consciousness independent of any definite human form and to attach it *immediately* to an *abstract* ideal which has no likeness.

Ahad Ha-Am then applies this essential difference to the very heart of the Gospels and drives his argument home in pungent terms.

Israel cannot accept with religious enthusiasm, as the word of God, the utterances of a man who speaks in his own name —not, 'Thus saith the Lord' but 'I say unto you'. This 'I' is in itself enough to drive Judaism away from the Gospels forever.

It would seem that the key to Ahad Ha-Am's estimation of the Gospels is his determination to counter what he thought to be the facile liberal creation of a superficial resemblance between Judaism and Christianity. Unfortunately he allows his aversion to run away with him. In his view the Jewish ethos can only be defined in terms of the deep-seated difference between the two faiths and opposition to all things Christian. He is far-sighted enough to realize that such particularity is opposed to universalistic aspiration and so he is quite content to occupy a mere 'corner of the world'. In an outlook such as this, where, he concludes, 'there is no room for compromise', there is all too often no room for variation, no room for the outsider in a meaningful and significant way, no room for a revelation of God in terms of person and certainly no room for a Jewish appreciation of Jesus. Happily, this is only one voice of modern Judaism and we should not forget that it is unfortunately also present in

100

some of the exclusive dogmatism of modern Christian theology.

There could hardly have been a more severe set-back to Ahad Ha-Am's policy of disengagement from all things Christian than the purposeful estimate of Jesus in the work of Joseph Klausner. His book *Jesus of Nazareth*, published in Jerusalem in 1922, was at first hardly noticed in the western world, partly because it was written in Hebrew and also because, at first sight, there was very little that was novel about it; yet when Herbert Danby translated Klausner's work into English in 1925 it caused a veritable storm in the Jewish world. By some it was heralded as an epoch-making book, while others were afraid that it constituted a most dangerous departure from the Jewish tradition. The fact that it has endured as the normative orthodox writing on Jesus seems to justify this sensation. Its genuine novelty can be traced in three directions: first, quite simply, that an orthodox Jew, a disciple of Ahad Ha-Am, an acknowledged leader of the new Jewish nationalism, devoted to the development of the *Yishuv* (the new Jewish settlement in Palestine), should have devoted such attention to the life of Jesus. Secondly, while it contained little that was new it was, in fact, a most able collation of previous Jewish appraisals of Jesus and his teachings and at the same time a competent synthesis of both Jewish and Christian scholarship on the original setting of the life and ministry of Jesus. Thirdly, it represented the most purposeful and thorough answer yet given to the perennial problem of why Jesus, who 'was a Jew and a Jew he remained until his last breath', and who played such a world-wide role, had been assigned such a meagre place in the Jewish tradition.

Although much of Klausner's answer follows a well-worn Jewish path, his distinctiveness lies in the way he was able to develop previous ideas and clothe them in a definitive manner. Other Jewish scholars had pointed to an unpatriotic emphasis in Jesus' teaching but none had defined the idea to the extent which Klausner achieved. He detects a serious denationalizing effect in the way in which Jesus 'so decries the value of the ceremonial laws as to make them of secondary importance to the moral laws and almost to nullify them'.[1] This was a dangerous distinction for Judaism in its ethnic implications. Klausner further noticed the seeds of national disintegration in the way in which Jesus isolated ethical considerations and often drove his demands to excessive conclusions that overrode all other considerations, be they the national oppression by Rome, or questions of inheritance or even marriage itself. In an oft-quoted passage, with a clarity reminiscent of Ahad Ha-Am, Klausner drives home his answer as to why Jesus and Judaism had to part.

Judaism is a national life, a life which the national religion and human ethical principles . . . embrace without engulfing. Jesus came and thrust aside all of the requirements of the national life; it was not that he set them apart and relegated them to their separate sphere in the life of the nation: he ignored them completely; in their stead he set up nothing but an ethico-religious system bound up with his conception of the Godhead. In the selfsame moment, he both annulled Judaism as the *life-force* of the Jewish nation and also the nation itself as a nation. . . . This inevitably brought it to pass that his people, Israel, rejected him. In its deeper con-

[1] *Jesus of Nazareth* (Eng. trans. by H. Danby, Allen and Unwin, 1925), p. 370.

sciousness the nation felt that then, more than at any other time, they must not be swallowed up in the great cauldron of nations in the Roman Empire, which were decaying for lack of God and of social morality (p. 390).

In conclusion, when Klausner asks the question: 'What is Jesus to the Jews?' his answer is in line with the main stream of Jewish tradition, which has consistently found some place for Jesus, even though it is radically different from the Christian evaluation. Klausner ends his book with these words:

To the Jewish nation he can be neither God nor the Son of God in the sense conveyed by belief in the Trinity. . . . Neither can they regard him as a Prophet . . . as a lawgiver or the founder of a new religion. . . . Neither is he a '*Tanna*' nor a Pharisaic Rabbi. . . . But Jesus is, for the Jewish nation, *a great teacher of morality and an artist in parable*. He is *the* moralist for whom, in the religious life, morality counts as— everything. . . . In his ethical code there is a sublimity, distinctiveness and originality in form unparalleled in any other Hebrew ethical code; neither is there any parallel to the remarkable art of his parables. The shrewdness and sharpness of his proverbs and his forceful epigrams serve, in an exceptional degree, to make ethical ideas a popular possession. If ever the day should come that this ethical code be stripped of its wrappings of miracles and mysticism, the Book of the Ethics of Jesus will be one of the choicest treasures in the literature of Israel for all time.

Beside the many side-effects of this great Jewish work, the one outstanding advance is that it gave a positive orthodox appreciation of Jesus' teaching. 'A great teacher of morality and an artist in parable' will always be remembered as Klausner's contribution, but nevertheless there remains some doubt as to the objectivity of his answer on Jesus' relation to the Jews. Did Klausner in attempting to penetrate the enigma of Jesus' strange relation to his own people transpose his own contemporary national predilections into the situation of Jesus' time? Was it not this *a priori* motivation that led Klausner to suggest that it was the subtle denationalizing tendency in Jesus' teaching which was the decisive factor why Jesus and his teaching was not accepted by the Jews of his or subsequent times? Our previous analysis of the events leading up to the separation of Judaism and Christianity demonstrate how complex the parting of the ways had been. Klausner no doubt isolated one of the causes of the division, but his emphasis that this had been primary is hardly vindicated by the facts.

A very marked advance on Klausner's appreciation of Jesus is evident in the novels dealing with Christian origins, particularly *The Nazarene*, written by Scholem Asch. They are the high water mark of a contemporary Jewish appreciation of Jesus. Where Scholem Asch improves on other writers is in the way in which he reopens the whole question of Jesus. It is a challenge to the entrenched attitudes of both Jews and Christians. Not only is Jesus seen as a thoroughly Jewish leader, but his appeal to Jews, be they ordinary people or distinguished rabbis like Gamaliel or Johanan ben Zakkai, is seen as far stronger than his conflicts with some of the Pharisees and Sadducees. Against such a background the trial and crucifixion are narrated as great tragedy.

Scholem Asch describes the unusual aspects of Jesus' person with great sympathy and even awe, but for the Christian reader it still sounds very different from the language to which he is accustomed in describing Jesus. It was and is an inner Jewish response to Jesus, and that in itself is most valuable. Perhaps his ethos communicates itself best when Asch is describing what Christians call the Incarnation and the Atonement. For him, while full of wonder, they are conceived in different terms.

> It seemed to me that the heavens covered themselves with glory and peace and good will descended to all men with the coming forth of the child. And I called to my husband: 'I know not how it is with me, but me seemeth that I see a great light, and singing reacheth my ears, and sweet odours like those of Eden surround me.'[1]

It would be a great mistake and misleading in the extreme to suggest that this view is that of the majority of Jews. The truth is rather that for many Scholem Asch's views are so extreme that they can hardly be regarded as Jewish at all. It is in fact in the reaction to modern Jewish studies of Jesus that a very different attitude to Jesus becomes apparent. Ahad Ha-Am's views emerge partly as a reaction to Claude Montefiore's liberal outlook. From his Zionist viewpoint Ahad Ha-Am was alarmed by the liberal Jewish tendency to assimilation; other more strictly religious Jews were equally alarmed by the direct path that seemed to lead from emancipation via assimilation to the baptismal font.

It is understandable that this breach in the Jewish community should be viewed with particular anxiety. Could it be possible that Jews who had resisted severe pressures, forced disputations, conversion and cruel ex-

[1] *The Nazarene*, Eng. trans. by Maurice Samuel (Routledge, London, and Putnam, New York, 1939), p. 257.

pulsions would now yield to the more subtle influence of a new-found liberty? One of the results of this was that in a sudden removal of barriers genuine differences were all too easily swept aside leading to a concentration on the more easily defined controversy over the person of Jesus. Indeed for many emancipated Jews the only crucial difference seemed to be 'the non-admission of Jesus'. When to this was added the further dilution of some Jewish admission of Jesus, it is not difficult to understand that it caused very real concern to the defenders of orthodoxy. It should not be forgotten that the great price of martyrdom and ghetto existence which orthodoxy had paid to preserve Jewish particularity now seemed to be in danger of becoming worthless. Consequently there arose a new 'tough' policy to deal with the issue which appeared to threaten the very survival of a distinctive Jewish community. This new resoluteness is well transmitted in an American Jewish weekly paper of the 1920s.

It is a proof of feebleness in many of our younger writers—the obvious pleasure they take in using words like 'crucifixion', 'Golgotha', and all that other class of word, apparently finding in them some sort of spiritual uplift. And the name of Jesus itself actually incites their pens to creative effort . . . they love the name. . . . If any of our day, even a Christian, approaches some creative idea and takes Jesus as subject in the old fashioned way, it only proves his limited outlook and stuffy mentality. *Jesus must never again even cross our minds.*[1]

Enough has already been said to demonstrate that this does not represent the historical Jewish attitude. It is perhaps an intensification of the old aloofness, but we see it in its true perspective as a hard party reaction to some

[1] *Ha-doar* (19 November 1926).

106

of the real dangers inherent in the liberal Jewish attitude to the Christian exploitation of the new Jewish openness in the emancipated era. It is a reaction fraught with fear lest the Jewish resistance against the Christian menace were to be in vain, and the threat of being swallowed up in a Gentile religion were at last to be realized. Such a fear that Jewry in the twentieth century stood in danger of extinction can be sensed in some of the great speeches of Chaim Weizmann. He and some of the other prophetic leaders of Zionism were convinced that the return to Palestine and the longed-for establishment of a Jewish state was 'either now or never'. All this is further underlined and illustrated when in 1962 Father Daniel (before his conversion Oswald Rufeisen), who feels himself a Jew despite his confession of the Christian faith, attempted to secure a ruling from the Israel High Court that, having been born a Jew, he should be allowed the right of every Jew to claim Israeli citizenship upon entry to the country. The refusal of the High Court and even more the crucial words of Justice Silberg indicate that the underlying anxiety of the above-quoted passage from *Ha-doar* had *not yet* passed, even though Father Daniel stood before the High Court of an independent sovereign Jewish state. Justice Silberg declared:

We were confronted at the outset, in this most unusual of cases, with the psychological paradox that we felt that we, as Jews, owed the petitioner, an apostate, all our admiration and thanks. For this man risked his own life times beyond number during the dark days of the Holocaust in Europe, to rescue his brother Jews from the very jaws of the Nazi beasts. It was difficult to envisage how such a man could be deprived of his life's aspiration to identify himself completely with the people

107

whom he loves and to become a citizen of the country of his dreams as of right, as a Jew, and not as an accepted stranger.

But we dared not allow our appreciation and gratitude to betray us into desecrating the name and content of the concept 'Jew'. For the petitioner has asked no less of us than to ignore the historical and sanctified meaning of the designation 'Jew' and to forget about those spiritual values for which we were massacred at various times during our long exile. If we are to accede to his request, the aura of glory and splendour surrounding our martyrs of the Middle Ages would pale and vanish without trace and our history would lose its continuity and begin to count its days from the beginning of the Emancipation, after the French Revolution. No man is entitled to demand such a sacrifice from us, even though he have as much to his credit as the petitioner.

Although the above undoubtedly represents the majority opinion, there was a dissident voice among the five judges. Justice Cohn expressed this disagreement in words that are at once restrained and yet reach out to the future. He declared:

If I have correctly understood my honourable colleague, he cannot, for historical reasons, ever envisage the possibility of regarding as a Jew a person who has allied himself to the Catholic Church, even though this Church is no longer, either in theory or in practice, an enemy of the Jewish people. I for my part, however, feel that change and progress are the very breath of historical continuity. The establishment of the State was a revolutionary event in the history of dispersed Israel. If in the Diaspora we have been either a tolerated or persecuted minority, in our own State we have become a nation like other nations, standing on our own feet. This revolution demands a change in values and in attitude, a revision in our diaspora thinking.

108

The Question of Jesus

The above words give form to an oft heard whisper during and after the 1962 trial—'*it was too soon*'. In Israel the day may yet come when Jesus can be seen by Jews apart from the terrible mask that the Gentile Church has constructed and fixed upon him in the time of her political and environmental supremacy.

The argument of this chapter can be summed up as follows: We have seen that in the earliest phase belief in Jesus was an open question among Jews. Consequent sharp theological controversy and Christian reaction to events from AD 66 to 135 brought about a separation of Church and Synagogue. This separation was extremely effective and only a minute knowledge of Jesus and his teaching is traceable in the normative Jewish writings of the Talmud. Although in the later sections of the Talmud some rabbis even confuse the designation and correct period of Jesus, at no point is his Jewishness denied. Almost the reverse is true for the teaching of Jesus. In the earliest Talmudic sources it is viewed as heretical, though some genuine rabbinic traits seem at first to be recognized. As the teaching of Jesus is more and more identified with the developing Christian doctrine, the charge of heresy becomes stronger until in the folklore of the Middle Ages it is seen as complete perversion.

At a later stage of the mediaeval period, mainly as a result of external pressure, there is a remarkable increase in the Jewish acquaintance with Christian doctrine and the New Testament. Maimonides and other Jewish thinkers concede that the spread of Christianity among the Gentiles is a benefit, since it unwittingly prepares the world for the Messianic Age by spreading at least a diluted form of the Torah throughout the world. Chris-

109

tian teaching may be a retrogressive step for Jews, but it contains sufficient Judaism for its success among the Gentiles to be viewed as an asset from the Jewish point of view. Jewish emancipation opened the way to a sharing in the new learning and culture of the west, which included participation in the current interest in Christian origins. On the Christian side Hebraists began to see the futility of much Christian evaluation of the Talmud, and Jewish scholars joined in and greatly added to the rediscovery that essentially Jesus was a Jew. It was some time before this new Jewish appreciation of Jesus was extended to his teaching. At first the value of Jesus' teaching was reduced to a mere diluted Judaism. Jewish scholars claimed that even such pinnacles as the Sermon on the Mount were borrowed Jewish property. Montefiore and to a lesser extent Klausner advanced from this position by admitting some new and positive value in Jesus' teaching. Scholem Asch perhaps more than any other Jewish writer dares to express an evaluation of Jesus from the inner angle of those who believe in him.

Almost in direct opposition to this new appreciation is a very different but nonetheless very significant Jewish reaction to Jesus. The new nationalism expressed by Ahad Ha-Am laid hold of the denationalizing effect of Jesus' teaching and thus tended to see Jesus as in direct opposition to the new national awareness. Similarly the very real danger of assimilation and conversion that followed in the wake of Jewish emancipation caused a reaction to Jesus, who was now viewed as the centre of all the forces that endangered the very survival of Judaism. Naturally but regrettably, this developed into seeing Jesus as the enemy, the original betrayer of

Judaism, the one who became a stranger and worse because he also became the magnet which drew other Jews into a betrayal of their heritage.

It can hardly be over-emphasized that this negative attitude cannot be dissociated from all the wrong in the Christian attitude and treatment of the Jews. It is only when we have recognized this all-important factor that we can possibly hope to place this Jewish evaluation in a correct perspective, and it is only against the acknowledgement of our disfigurement of Jesus that we dare to suggest points of deficiency in the Jewish vision of Jesus. First, this is evident in the meagre knowledge of Jesus that lies behind the sparse reference to him in the Talmud. Secondly, there is the very restricted way in which the teaching of Jesus is seen only in its dissected parts rather than as a whole; and, thirdly, there is the total lack of any awareness of the Jesus of inner experience. It may, of course, be questioned whether such an awareness is at all possible other than from the standpoint of Christian experience, but this is to give greater finality to the Christian interpretation of Jesus than to Jesus himself. It is one thing to see this whole dimension almost wholly lacking in the Jewish appreciation of Jesus but it is quite another matter to suggest that, if this deficiency is ever made good, then it must equal the Christian experience and interpretation.

The situation at the present time seems to be that Christians need to recognize that they dare not prejudge what would be the content and interpretation of a full Jewish encounter with Jesus, and Jews should not necessarily preclude the possibility of the truth of the Christian affirmation about Jesus in such an encounter. This is asking for a degree of objectivity that neither Christians nor Jews have so far reached. Christians need to be particularly cautious not to read their own desire for a deepening of the Jewish understanding of Jesus into any and every Jewish acknowledgement of some deficiency in their estimate of Jesus. We have already referred to Rabbi Maurice Eisendrath's challenge for a new Jewish appraisal of Jesus. This challenge has not yet been worked out. In Israel, there are at present only inarticulate rumblings here and there but perhaps the most hopeful sign is the way in which Jesus is beginning to be reclaimed as a Jewish seer native to the Holy Land. Only when Christians allow and help this reclamation to be secure can we hope for a Jewish encounter with Jesus that will look him in the face and not be ashamed. The poetic words of a Jewish woman to a Christian friend express this thought most poignantly:

> There is something between us now;
> The cry you did not raise.
>
> You have washed your hands again.
> Put down the pitcher.
> This water will flow between us.
>
> Give me back Jesus;
> He is my brother.
> He will walk with me
> Behind the grey ghetto wall
> Into the slaughter-house.
> I will lead him into the lethal chamber;
> He will lie down upon the poisoned stone;
> The little children pricked with the death bubble
> Will come unto him.

The Question of Jesus

Return to him the yellow badge.
Give me back Jesus;
He is not yours.[1]

These words make demands on all of us, but in view of past relationships it would certainly seem to be the right thing for Christians to take the first step in seeking not only to correct the past but to go on to an inner appreciation of Judaism, for we need to listen and understand before ever we can hope that the person at the centre of our faith can be understood.

[1] By Marie Syrkin, quoted in *Verdict on Father Daniel* (a Parkes Library Pamphlet, Royston, Herts, 1963).

113

4

The Message of Judaism

>>>◆<<<

How sweet are thy words unto my taste! Yea, sweeter than honey to my mouth. *Psalm 119.103*

Unless Thy Law had been my delight, I should then have perished in mine affliction (Ps. 119.92). The children of Israel said: 'But for Thy Torah which was with me and was my delight I should then have perished in mine affliction.' Likewise Moses said: 'When my cares are many within me, Thy comforts delight my soul' (Psalm 94.19). When Pharaoh said: 'Let heavier work be laid upon the men, that they may labor therein; and let them not delight in lying words' (Ex. 5.9), he had in mind that the children of Israel owned books in whose words they took delight from Sabbath to Sabbath. Hence it is said 'Unless Thy Law had been my delight, I should then have perished in mine affliction.' *Midrash on Psalm 119*[1]

WE turn now from the battlefield of Christian-Jewish polemics to a humble listening-in to what Judaism has to say to us as Christians. What exactly is involved by such 'listening-in' can by no means be taken for granted. Recently a Christian professor suggested to a Jewish colleague in Jerusalem that there should be an exchange

[1] Eng. trans. by W. G. Braude (Yale University Press, New Haven, 1959), vol. II, p. 272.

of theological teaching between their respective universities. After all, he argued, it would surely be a good thing for the Hebrew University in Jerusalem to hear what a Christian theologian had to say. Equally, he maintained, it would be beneficial for Christians in his university to have a Jewish theologian in their midst. When the Jewish professor pressed for actual details, his Christian counterpart suggested that a Christian theologian should be invited to the Hebrew University for a whole academic year, but he thought it would be sufficient to have the Jewish theologian at a six weeks' summer course. That is not humble listening!

There are many Christian books that attempt to describe Judaism with much the same kind of 'built-in advantage' for the Christian point of view. Even when the great rabbinical concepts are being discussed, it is invariably from the standpoint of where Judaism approaches or strengthens Christian ideas. Genuine 'humble listening-in' asks 'What can I as a Christian learn from the truth that God has given to the Jewish people and faith and that they have maintained throughout the centuries?' Unpopular as the fact may be, there cannot be any intelligent 'listening-in to Judaism' without at least being aware of the primary sources. The primary source of Judaism is not the Old Testament but the Old Testament plus its rabbinical interpretation. An outline account of these sources, that does not attempt much more than an explanation of titles, is given in Appendix II.

It would certainly be proper and orderly (though the rabbis were no lovers of order) to commence our 'listening in to Judaism' with some account of the great Jewish affirmation of God in the declaration of the *Shema*,[1] but, as Christians are still unaccustomed to listen to Rabbinic Judaism we might become more rightly attuned if we consider first the rabbinic concept of *Shechina*. Is it not true that when we think positively of the rabbis' idea of God, we may be prepared to concede that they stress God's transcendence and otherness, that their reticence in refusing to pronounce God's Name is a pointer to their great awe of the Holy One, but we usually qualify all this by implying that God was a distant deity for the rabbis? We rightly spot the danger that their lofty conception of God could all too easily have led to a cold deism, but this was not allowed to become a serious danger in Judaism. At the very centre of the rabbis' religion was their conviction of God's special relation to Israel, of his will declared in the Torah for all the contingencies of life, and even of a particular doctrine of his presence, known as the *Shechina*, that far predates the contemporary theological popularity of the 'presence' idea. Such a religion could be at once strictly monotheistic and most naturally develop a profound understanding of God's immanence or of his real presence among men. The rabbis as inheritors of the Old Testament did not have to invent the notion that God was present with his people Israel, for Judaism begins with God's approach to and presence with a people; apart from that presence it would never have originated, and even if it had, it would certainly not have survived. Moses expressed this almost at the beginning

[1] Simply meaning 'Hear!' which is the first word in the Deuteronomic affirmation of God: 'Hear, O Israel, the Lord our God, the Lord is one' (Deut. 6.4), which epitomizes the rabbinic belief in and hold upon monotheism.

116

of the great Jewish adventure; 'If thy presence go not with me, carry us not up hence' (Ex. 33.15).

The Old Testament, although it does not itself use the term *Shechina*, speaks with a rich and manifold diversity about God's presence that works up to the great climax of God's ubiquity in Psalm 139. The rabbis, in the same way as the writers of the New Testament, laid hold upon, developed and extended certain images of God's presence in the Old Testament, which they saw as an assurance and guarantee that God was and would remain present with them. Just as the distinctive Christian symbols of Christ's real presence in his Church do not originate that presence but are concrete tokens that he is there, so similarly the *Shechina* verified God's presence in Israel. Etymologically *Shechina* has the meaning of 'dwelling among', 'covering up' and 'hovering over'. In a sentence George Knight expressed it as 'the majestic presence and manifestation of God which has descended to dwell amongst men'.

The most impressive visual expression of this idea in the Old Testament is the tabernacle in the wilderness with the 'pillar of cloud' hovering over the sanctuary as concrete evidence of God's localized presence.

Closely related to the image of the tabernacle is 'the pillar of cloud' and 'the pillar of fire' that led the Israelites through the wilderness. Here, to the idea of God's visible presence we have the added sense of God's manifest guidance. We might express this in another way, by saying that as the *Shechina* is God's presence made real, so it naturally extends to the effects of such a presence. God appears in the *Shechina* not only to confront, but also to speak and direct. Another effect of his presence is to display his glory. So we find that the idea of God's glory is never far removed from that of his presence, indeed, there are occasions when the rabbis use the two Hebrew words *Shechina* and *Kavod* (glory) interchangeably. Nowhere is this connection so closely worked out as in the New Testament, where the Greek word *Doxa*, usually translated glory, has often to do the duty for both Hebrew words, *Shechina* and *Kavod*. This is particularly evident in St John's Gospel, for the disciples who are aware of God's presence in the life of Jesus are at the same moment exposed to his glory: 'And the Word was made flesh and dwelt among us (and we beheld his glory, the glory as of the only begotten of the Father) full of grace and truth' (John 1.14).

But to return to the rabbinical expressions for the *Shechina*, we should note the use they made of the fundamental elements of 'light' and 'fire' which in conjunction with 'high mountains' are most primitive symbols[1] of God's presence and are also freely employed in both Old and New Testaments. It is therefore hardly surprising that the *Shechina* in the thought of the rabbis should at first be associated with material objects, but this occupies only a subsidiary place in their thinking. As they developed their doctrine of the *Shechina* they increasingly moved away from a concrete but visible manifestation associated with material objects to one conditioned by moral and spiritual qualities. Perhaps the most well known and typical rabbinical example of this is the association of the *Shechina* with those who study the Torah.

---

[1] Cf. Michael Ramsey, *The Glory of God and the Transfiguration of Christ* (Longmans, London, 1949), and especially ch. 2, 'The History of a Word'.

118

The Message of Judaism

In the Mishna (the earliest and most authoritative section of the Talmud) Rabbi Hanina ben Teradion of the mid-second century said: 'If two sit together and words of Torah are between them, the Shechinah rests between them' (*Anthology*, p. 23).[1] The similarity to Matthew 18.20 is too striking for any Christian writer, including the present one, to allow it to pass unnoticed. Closely related to this idea is the association of the *Shechina* with pious Israelites as expressed in a terse sentence of Rabbi Simeon ben Yohai: 'Whithersoever the righteous go, the Shechinah goes with them' (*Anthology*, p. 85). The reverse of this idea is that a loss of the *Shechina* results through involvement in sin, and this is lyrically expressed by the rabbis in an oft-quoted midrash (a rabbinical interpretation) on Numbers (*Anthology*, p. 84).

We may note here a great similarity to the Christian doctrine of the indwelling Spirit in the life of the saints. Such a concept was not unknown to the rabbis. At times their thought on the *Shechina* approached very near to that of an indwelling presence, and just as in the New Testament the concept of the 'indwelling Christ' is at times interchangeable with the 'indwelling Spirit', so likewise in rabbinical thought there is no hard line drawn between their doctrine of the Holy Spirit (*Ruah ha Kodesh*) and the *Shechina*. Indeed, the two concepts often merge into each other. As sin drives away the *Shechina* so

[1] Wherever possible, quotations from the rabbinical sources are taken from *A Rabbinic Anthology* by C. G. Montefiore and H. Loewe (Macmillan, 1938, reissued by Meridian Books, New York, 1960), cited throughout this chapter as *Anthology*. This book is by far the best introduction to the 'sea of the Talmud' and, for those who wish to study further, it conveniently gives the references to the primary sources.

likewise the Holy Spirit does not abide with the 'idle', or, in the words of a midrash on Psalm 24.3 (*Anthology*, p. 202), 'The Holy Spirit does not rest where there is idleness or sadness or ribaldry, or frivolity, or empty speech, but only where there is joy.' Without the slightest distortion of rabbinical thought we could substitute the term *Shechina* for 'the Holy Spirit' in this midrash.

So far we have not mentioned the obvious thought of the *Shechina* as having some kind of mediatory role between God and Israel. This aspect naturally interested Christian theologians, especially as ideas similar to those about the effects of the *Shechina* are employed by the New Testament writers to express their thought on the relation of Jesus to God. The most striking instance of this is in the prologue of St John's Gospel, where the author uses the kernel thought of *Shechina* as the visible expression of God's presence among men and applies it directly to the incarnation: 'And the Word became flesh and dwelt among us' (John 1.14).

At this point however we need to be on our guard against losing the true perspective of this rabbinical concept by evaluating it from the viewpoint of how it approximates to related Christian ideas. If for instance we are on the look-out to see whether the rabbis at any time so personified the *Shechina* as to approach the idea of a mediator, we shall not be disappointed, but we may be and in this instance certainly are as far off the mark of their true thought as a non-Christian theologian who painstakingly extracted all the available New Testament utterances that in any way limit Jesus and then on this evidence proceeded to construct what he thought to be the New Testament doctrine of the Lord Christ! The rabbis were not particularly concerned with the precise relation of the *Shechina* to God and even less with the strict definition of this relationship. Almost the reverse is true for our New Testament writers, who were particularly interested in the relationship of Jesus to the Father, yet they like the rabbis prefer to state such elusive truth in pliable subtleties rather than in restrictive and definitive terms. So we may note that at one moment the rabbis may allow themselves the extravagance of speaking as though the *Shechina* had a separate existence, but this is just as likely to be followed by another statement of God's indivisible unity and direct approach to men. As Rabbi Joshua of Sikhnin expressed it:

The matter is like a cave which lies by the seashore: the tide rises, and the cave becomes full of water, but the sea is no whit less full. So the sanctuary and the tent of meeting were filled with the radiance of Shechinah, but the world was no less filled with God's glory (*Anthology*, p. 15).

This brings us back to the original emphasis of the rabbis in their bold insistence on the special relationship of the *Shechina* to Israel. It is the one thing needful for us to recognize. We may be forgiven for not knowing every shade of the rabbinic meaning of the *Shechina*, but this one dimension, the unique relation of the *Shechina* to Israel, at once a people and a religion, is a most decisive factor in our evaluation of the Jewish people and faith. The rabbis never seem to tire in their contemplation of this truth. They revel in discovering a hundred and one different vantage points for expressing the depth and richness of God's abiding presence with his people Israel. In an almost breath-taking thought they liken the

121

descent of the *Shechina* to Israel as no less significant than
the creation of the world (cf. *Anthology*, p. 82). Even
more striking than this idea is the great subtlety of rabbinic thought when they dare to suggest that not even
sin and uncleanness itself is able to wrench the *Shechina*
from Israel. It is not that the rabbis are going back on
their conviction that the *Shechina* is conditioned by moral
and spiritual qualities, that sin inevitably drives the
Shechina away, but rather that they cannot believe that
in a people whom God has chosen, to whom he entrusts
his very reputation in the world (related to *Kiddush ha-
Shem*, that is 'Sanctification of the Name'), sin can never
become the primary and decisive factor in their community life. The rabbis were aware of the real and terrible failings of Israel but they were even more confident
in a God who looked upon Israel in a totality that sees
beyond the moment of a particular relapse into sin and
uncleanness to the measure in which Israel has lived and
will yet live up to her high calling in God's overall purpose and plan for this world. From a perspective that
viewed the descent of the *Shechina* to Israel as being as
decisive as the creation itself, it was totally inconceivable
that within the context of this world anything could loom
so large as to effect the departure of the *Shechina* from
Israel. A Midrash on Numbers expresses this in unequi-
vocal terms:

Beloved are the Israelites to God, for even when they are
unclean the Shechinah dwells among them (Num. 5.2, 3)
(*Anthology*, p. 64).

The line of thought in this and other similar sayings
seems to answer the taunt that the exile and suffering of

122

Israel demonstrates that God has forsaken them, that their relationship to him has been broken. The rabbis faced this taunt, but with strong faith prefer to view the sufferings of their people as a deep mystery of the ways of God with Israel, and even if in part it is a chastisement from a Father to his children, it is in no sense an end to God's covenant with Israel, it is never a withdrawal of the *Shechina*.

Lest we should feel that this flight of rabbinic thought has no foundation in the Bible, we can hardly do better than to conclude our contemplation of the *Shechina* with some thought on the call of Moses at the burning bush recorded in Ex. 3.2-5. Although this incident lends itself to almost limitless allegorization, of a kind so foreign and unattractive to us but so greatly favoured and employed by the rabbis, their exposition here, allowing for this tendency, is strangely reserved. The Midrash Exodus Rabba on this passage (Soncino edition, p. 53) takes up what must have been a leading question on its interpretation at that time. 'Why the thorn bush?' It gives us the answer in a typical rabbinic anecdote:

A heathen once asked R. Joshuah b. Karhah: 'Why did God choose a thorn bush from which to speak to Moses?' He replied: 'Were it a carob tree or a sycamore tree, you would have asked the same question; but to dismiss you without any reply is not right, so I will tell you why. To teach you that no place is devoid of God's presence, not even a thorn bush.'

With increasing penetration the Midrash goes on to elucidate the extraordinary symbol of a burning bush (Soncino edition, p. 55):

Because he (Moses) had thought to himself that the Egyptians might consume Israel; hence did God show him a fire which burned but did not consume, saying to him: 'Just as the thorn bush is burning and is not consuming, so the Egyptians will not be able to destroy Israel.'

Even more telling is the terse answer in the Midrash Leviticus Rabba (Soncino edition, p. 140) where Moses asked: 'Why is not the bush burnt away?' He was given the succinct reply: 'Because my glory is present therein.' It would be extremely strange if with such primary symbols of the *Shechina* as 'light', 'fire', and even a 'high mountain' the rabbis had not directly identified the symbols in this passage with the *Shechina*, and of course they did. Returning to the Midrash on this passage which comments on the phrase 'IN A FLAME OF FIRE' we read (Soncino edition, p. 53):

At first an angel acted as intermediary and stood in the centre of the fire, and afterwards the Shechinah descended and spoke with him from the midst of the thorn bush.

The rabbinical comment on this passage speaks with a single voice. The varied symbols of these six verses are kaleidoscoped together so that we see only one multi-coloured picture in which the splendour of God's presence in the flame of fire and the uncommon burning of a most common thorn bush are so at one that we see both as indistinguishable. Israel by itself is no more unusual than the thorn bush in the wilderness, but because the *Shechina* cannot be separated from her she can never be destroyed. Here is a genuine clue why the Synagogue has persisted alongside the emergence of the Church, and at the same time the exposure of what has been so sadly amiss in our approach to Israel. The moment that we recognize that the unextinguishable life of Israel is nothing less than the indestructible presence of God in her midst, our attitude to the Jewish people and faith undergoes a most radical change. We are ourselves present at the burning bush and hear the words 'Put off thy shoes from off thy feet'—words that can only mean one thing, to step down from a position of superiority and to remove the conceit and high-handed manner that has so largely characterized the Christian approach to Judaism in the past and so make our approach in the deep humility symbolized by bare feet. The comment of the Midrash on the above words that 'Wherever the Shechina appears one must not go about with shoes on' extends the demand for humility to be co-extensive in the whole area of the contemporary Christian-Jewish relationship.

We turn now to the characteristic rabbinic word for the affirmation of God—the *Shema*.[1] As other Jewish prayers, benedictions and scriptural passages that are usually referred to by their opening word or phrase, *Shema*, meaning 'hear' is the first word of the great Jewish declaration of God:

'Hear O Israel, the Lord our God, the Lord is one.'

This is undoubtedly the earliest proclamation of monotheism. It is part of a larger statement in Deut. 6.4-9, which very early in the history of Jewish worship was extended to include two other scriptural passages, Deut. 11.13-21 and Num. 15.37-41. The content of these passages is very different from what we might expect of a basic statement of God's nature. The simplest explanation

---

[1] Cf. the second chapter, 'God—There is none Save He' in Kenneth Cragg's penetrating study on Islam, *The Call of the Minaret* (Oxford University Press, 1956).

is that the *Shema* is not a Jewish parallel to the Apostles' Creed, indeed in some sense it approximates more to the significant place occupied by the 'Our Father' in Christian worship. The use, structure and content of the *Shema* are essentially a part of Jewish worship, they are an expression of the experience of God, the God that the first sentence so boldly declares. We need here to distinguish between the essential affirmation of God made in the one staggering sentence and the way that this is linked and developed to the composite statement comprising the *Shema*. It will be convenient for our purpose to comment first on the rabbinic explanation of this affirmation of God, but it is essential that we keep in mind that the very structure and content of the Shema point to the rabbinic emphasis that God is known and acknowledged in experience, and this experience centres in the proper observance of religion. This is most impressively borne out in the Jewish emphasis upon 'doing' rather than 'believing'. It is not that this doing has ever been viewed as an antithesis to believing but rather as the complete expression of a committed belief.

This particular ethos of Judaism strikes a non-Jewish visitor to Israel perhaps more than any other religious feature of the modern Jewish state. Time and again this sentiment has been expressed by a perplexed tourist or pilgrim. 'Why all this emphasis on doing this or that?' 'Surely religion is a matter of the heart, of what one believes and not the keeping of external regulations?' It is certainly difficult for anyone unfamiliar with this fundamental attitude in Judaism in appreciate why religious authorities in Israel should be so insistent that all kinds of seeming trivialities, such as for instance the fixing of a *mezuza* (a glass, wood or metal case containing the first two paragraphs of the shema from Deut. 6.4-9 and 11.13-21) on the entrance of every Jewish house or office, should be scrupulously carried out. It goes without saying that this emphasis on externals has its dangers, but it also has its most valuable securities. It demonstrates not so much Judaism's hold and belief on God but rather the extent of Judaism's commitment to the living God.

All this should serve to warn the Christian reader of the very different approach of the rabbis in their thought and language about God to that prevalent in the Christian tradition. While undoubtedly the powerfully suggestive words 'Hear O Israel, the Lord our God, the Lord is One' fulfil a credal purpose in Judaism, they were not developed in the set form that similar statements in the New Testament were employed in the formulation of Christian creeds. It has always been somewhat of a disappointment to dogmatic theologians that the rabbis of the Talmudic era produced neither a developed creed nor even a precise treatise on the nature of God. Not only is there this absence of a developed credal form but also an absence of the technical language that Christian theologians employ in developing their concept of God. Terms so dear to Christian theologians as transcendent, imminent, omniscient, omnipotent and omnipresent appear to have no appeal to the rabbis. Such concepts do enter Jewish thinking with the mediaeval Jewish philosophers, of whom Maimonides is the outstanding example. His thirteen articles of belief, particularly his first four of God as creator, of his unity, inseparability and eternity are in their form much nearer to Christian theological language than the rabbis' comment on the *Shema* and related statements on God's nature.

The issue is not a simple one. Besides a divergence in method it raises the clash between Greek and Hebrew forms of thought. More directly it is explained by the fact that Maimonides worked out his articles of belief under the stress of a dominant non-Jewish culture and setting. It is not surprising therefore that there have always been Jewish critics of Maimonides who have taken strong issue with his thirteen articles of belief, not so much on the ground of their content but more on that of their particular form and the idea that assent to a formulated statement of belief has an essential place in Jewish orthodoxy. This is viewed as a serious departure from the much looser and incidental method of expressing Jewish belief generally employed by the rabbis. On this point the rabbis are both attractive and instructive—attractive on account of their flexible expression about God, instructive in their simple yet firm hold upon monotheism. It is to their credit that they did not impede their declaration about God with long and intricate definitions and yet that their belief in the direct monotheism expressed by the *Shema* was absolutely fundamental to their life and religion. The rabbis were not greatly troubled to substantiate their belief in the existence of God, yet at almost every stage of Jewish history their particular concept of monotheism has been challenged. To the rabbis their belief in one God was so fundamental that they spoke of it as the very origin of their people and religion. Undoubtedly they were aware of the many ways in which their pre-exilic forebears were untrue to the affirmation of one God in the *Shema*. Yet they could not conceive of claiming Abraham

The Message of Judaism

for their father without ascribing to him the acknowledgement of the same monotheism that they affirmed
in the *Shema* (cf. *Anthology*, p. 12).

There is little speculation in the opening sentence of
the *Shema*, but we are able to deduce three simple truths
about God on which the rabbis love to dwell and muse.
They do not state this in a credal manner but their
writings abound with their comment and thought on
these three simple truths. First, that their God is the only
God; second, that his nature is essentially a unity; and
third, that he bears a special relationship to Israel. It is
true that one would have to read a considerable amount
of the Talmud and Midrash to illustrate this, but here as
elsewhere we are greatly indebted to Montefiore and
Loewe for the way in which they have collated the available material in their *Anthology*. The Midrash Rabba on
Deuteronomy (*Anthology*, p. 23) shows how straightforward the rabbis can be in their defence of monotheism.
Their direct appeal to the ineffectiveness of inanimate
objects as a conclusive argument against idols may seem
somewhat naive to us, but we can hardly doubt that it
must have been a cogent argument in its original setting:

R. Judah b. Simon said: 'An idol is near and far; God is
far and near.' 'How?' 'An idolater makes an idol, and sets it
up in his house. So the idol is near. But one may cry unto
the idol, and it will not answer, therefore the idol is far. But
God is far and near.' 'How?' R. Judah b. Simon said: 'From
here to heaven is a journey of five hundred years: therefore
God is far; but He is also near, for if a man prays and medi-
tates in his heart, God is near to answer his prayer.'

But the rabbis are not always so direct and straight-

129

forward even when they are speaking of the pre-eminence of monotheism. When the rabbis speak of God's unity they are quite able to state this categorically without any asides as is the case in the Midrash Rabba on Leviticus (*Anthology*, p. 120):

Therefore we hope in Him, we wait for Him, and we confess the Unity of His Name twice a day, as we repeat the words, 'Hear, O Israel, the Lord our God, the Lord is One' (Deut. 6.4).

However, on numerous other occasions the rabbis' exposition of God's unity is anything but direct. Not only do they employ a great variety of allegorical interpretations, but also most unpromising verses of scripture are pressed into use. This is also true of the Christian arguments for the concept of Trinity which have been substantiated by proof-texts from both the Old and New Testaments. It might well be—though we shall never know—that if the rabbis' concept of God's unity had not been challenged by the Christian doctrine of the Trinity then the rabbis might not have troubled to define what they meant by God's unity, but there can be no doubt that they would have held the conviction that 'the Lord is one' just as strongly. The plain facts of history are that the rabbis were continually challenged in their affirmation of absolute monotheism. Just as the original statement of the *Shema* is in some sense a contradiction of polytheism, so many of the ways in which the rabbis expound their concept of God's unity contradict this or that assailant of their belief. At one time the rabbis may be greatly disturbed by the popularity of some kind of gnostic dualism, and so they have to go out of their way

The Message of Judaism

to assert that God's unity does not admit any secondary power. On another occasion they may be challenged by the gnostic speculation of a whole hierarchy of intermediaries, and so at that time they declare that God needs no viceroy in his approach to Israel, that he is able to speak directly with man. Of particular interest to Christians is of course the rabbis' defence of God's unity when they are obviously guarding against the Christian concept of Trinity. There could hardly be a clearer statement of this intention than in the Midrash Rabba on Exodus (*Anthology*, p. 12):

> R. Abbahu said: 'An earthly king has a father, a brother or a son; with God it is not so. For God says, "I am the first, for I have no father; I am the last, for I have no brother; and there is no god beside me, for I have no son" (Isa. 44.6).'

The real issue here is whether this can be taken as a fair criticism of the Christian understanding of Jesus' divine sonship, or whether it is merely effective against a degraded and popular form of the Christian belief of the second person of the Trinity. Claude Montefiore in his *Anthology* (p. 7) generously admits that the rabbis never really understood the Christian doctrine of the Trinity. He writes:

> I have not come across any passage which seriously tackles the Christian conception of the Trinity, or which attempts to show that a Unity, which is a simple and pure Unity, is a higher or truer conception of the divine nature than a Unity of a Trinity or than a Trinity in a Unity. Where the Rabbis reply to the *minim* (heretics, sectaries, and sometimes Christians), they always represent these *minim* as believing in many gods. In other words, the doctrine of the Trinity (if

that is referred to) is construed to mean Tritheism, which indeed was, and perhaps still is, its vulgar corruption.

Now it is not difficult for Christians to admit that the doctrine of the Trinity was often in popular form degraded to nothing more than a belief in three gods and that to this was occasionally added a goddess. But it is only fair that we should go on to ask whether the Christian Fathers in their formulation of the orthodox doctrine of the Trinity ever really understood the rabbinic doctrine of the unity of God. It would be presumptuous and premature to attempt an answer on this issue, but at least we can recognize the problem. The Christian Church is committed to the belief in 'Jesus as Lord' but it is surely no less committed to the uncompromising monotheism of the *Shema*. It has never been easy for Christian theologians to reconcile these two beliefs. Is it too much to ask that in our contemporary search for a meaningful Christology we should once more place ourselves under the instruction of the original teachers of monotheism? Indeed, is this not what is involved in a 'humble listening-in to Judaism'?

Perhaps it was unavoidable that in the past Christian interest in the way the rabbis expounded God's unity centred its attention on those aspects of the rabbis' teaching that were directly contradicting the Christian belief in Trinity. It was emphasized that the rabbinical teaching here was a mere reaction to Christian teaching. The other point of Christian concentration seems to have been in those instances where the rabbis' unguarded language either on the Holy Spirit, the personification of Wisdom or the *Shechina* seemed to leave a loophole to squeeze in the Christian concept of Trinity. It is not surprising that this type of inquiry missed much of the most character-istic rabbinic teaching of God's unity. The heart of the rabbis' conviction on the nature of that unity is much deeper than a mere restriction to a mathematical unity and goes beyond the way in which they defended that unity against this or that heresy. It would appear that the rabbis wrestled with some of the basic problems that arise directly out of the concept of God's unity. Is this aspect of the divine nature like any other single human unity? Can God's unity be reduced to the comprehensible unity of a human individual? Does not God's uniqueness extend also to the way that we can understand his unity?

The training and practice of continual discussion made the rabbis great masters in the manipulation of language and argument and thus made them well able to answer their opponents. While they may not have faced the above questions in the form in which we have expressed them, in a way they do indicate that they were not un-aware of them for they are prepared to admit their own limitations. There is a most attractive subtlety in the way the rabbis can maintain and declare uncompromisingly God's absolute unity and yet indicate that their under-standing and language is inadequate to compass the nature of God (cf. *Anthology*, p. 21).

Developing this line of thought the rabbis realized that all the tools at their disposal were in the last resort in-adequate. The highest human activity, the most carefully chosen language, even the biblical imagery about God, all were limited. This in no sense diminishes their hold on monotheism; rather it enhances it. They shrink from the idolatrous presumption that their definition can ever circumscribe God. He who cannot be contained in imagery or picture can neither be framed in language, formula, or idea (cf. *Anthology*, pp. 32-33).

So far we have elaborated some of the ways in which the rabbis emphasized that their God is the only God and that his nature is a unique unity. We turn now to consider the great stress that they place on the special link between this God and Israel. The rabbis have often been accused of making God the special possession of the Jews. No one can deny that the rabbis claim that the one true and living God had a special relationship to the people Israel, but this never meant for the rabbis that there were other gods or that their God was unconcerned with other nations. Among rabbinical sayings that illustrate this point the most famous and oft-quoted occurs in the Mishna (*Anthology*, p. 52):

The ministering angels wanted to sing a hymn at the destruction of the Egyptians, but God said: 'My children lie drowned in the sea, and you would sing?'

It is undoubtedly true that the rabbis did over-emphasize the unique link between God and Israel, yet it must be said in their favour that they did not invent the idea; it was built upon the Old Testament concept of the Covenant. Apart from this idea it is difficult to conceive how a true relationship between God and a people could have developed. It is greatly to the credit of the rabbis that, given the unique link between God and a people, they should have developed this in terms of the full and satisfying relationship that exists within a family (cf. *Anthology*, p. 62).

For our particular interest we have attempted to trace some of the rabbis' comments on their concept of monotheism so clearly enunciated in the opening sentence of the *Shema*. We should, however, be on our guard against superimposing our tidy approach on the rabbis' unsystematic method. The rabbis have other great words which emphasize various aspects of their understanding of God. So *Malkut Shamayim* (literally the 'Kingdom of Heaven' but more properly 'God's Kingly Rule') expresses the rabbis' great stress on God's sovereignty, *Kiddush Ha-Shem* (the 'Sanctification of the Name') emphasizes Israel's responsibility toward God as the trustee of his reputation in the world, and *Yirat Shamayim* (the 'Fear of Heaven') stresses the awe and deference that is God's due.

It would certainly never have occurred to the rabbis that their understanding of God had to be contained in such terms or that these terms could be treated separately. They pass from one concept to the other with great ease for they are all interrelated.

For us moderns it is the simplicity of their enunciation of monotheism in the *Shema* that is attractive, but this does not mean that the rabbis did not face the many questions about God that lie behind so much of the traditional Christian theological language. If the rabbis had not been concerned with such problems as how a transcendent God can at the same time be intimately related and even involved in this world, if they had never been faced with the paradox of an all-seeing and all-knowing God who at the same time allows the exercise of free will, we might well think that their immunity to such problems precludes them from being of any help to us today. The rabbis did face these questions but they never pretended to solve them. Their way of approach is of real

value for it is less set than the Christian formulas and full
of indications that these questions admit only of an
approach and not of a complete answer. We can almost
feel the way in which they struggle with the problem of
transcendence and immanence, as is evident in a Midrash
on Psalm 90 (*Anthology*, pp. 19-20):

> R. Jose b. Halafta said: 'We should not know if God were
> an appendage to the world, or if the world were His appen-
> dage, had not He Himself said, "Behold, there is a place by
> me" (Ex. 33.21). He is the place of the world (i.e. He includes
> the world): the world is not His place. So the world is an
> appendage to Him; He is not an appendage to the world.'

It would certainly go beyond the evidence to suggest that
the rabbis shared our new-found sensitivity about speaking of God in spatial language, yet they do seem to
realize that God transcends their own restricted spatial
experience; at least this seems to be conveyed by a Midrash on Psalm 24 (*Anthology*, pp. 15-16):

> R. Phinehas said: 'If an earthly king is in his bedchamber,
> he is not in his dining-room, and *vice versa*, but God fills the
> upper and lower regions at one and the same time, as it is
> said, "His glory is over the earth and the heaven" (Ps. 148.13)
> and, "Do I not fill heaven and earth?" (Jer. 23.24).'

Montefiore, commenting on this aspect of rabbinical
thought (*Anthology*, p. 19), suggests that here the rabbis
even go beyond the great Old Testament expression of
God's ubiquity found in Psalm 139. In their effort to
express the inadequacy of their world as in any way containing God or being able to measure or comprehend him,
they suggest, as we have seen in the Midrash on Psalm 90

136

just quoted, that 'the world is an appendage to Him. He is not an appendage to the world.' It is strangely reminiscent of William Temple's dictum:

$$\text{God} - \text{the world} = \text{God; the world} - \text{God} = 0.$$

The rabbis further developed this idea by a strange device in which they refer to God as 'the place'. This seems yet another way in which the rabbis confess the inadequacy of relating God to anything within their experience and so as a last resort they suggest that we must reverse the process and relate all we know to God (cf. *Anthology*, pp. 20-21).

In a somewhat different way when the rabbis wrestled with the problem of how Israel's conduct can possibly affect God's image in the world, an idea which lies behind the concept of *Kiddush Ha-Shem*, they dared to suggest that the practice of their religion had a direct effect on God. Yet it seems that no sooner had they said this than they became aware that this could not be the whole truth, there remained an area even in this aspect of their understanding of God that they could not comprehend (cf. *Anthology*, p. 35).

It would be rash in the extreme to arrive at hard and fast conclusions on the particular trend of rabbinic thought just outlined. While no one can doubt the rabbis' firm belief in one God, his unity, and his special relation to Israel, it does seem that in their further definition of God they were acutely aware of the inadequacy of their language, their experience, their understanding and their whole world and so they wisely avoided the language of strict definition and preferred to use more elastic language and a great diversity of imagery. At times their

137

expression was rather crude, often they were excessive in the use of their imagination, but the genuine way in which they allowed for their varied limitations meant that their language about God did not restrict him within the competence of their understanding, world or definition.

At the beginning of our comment on the *Shema* we stressed the essential framework of this affirmation of God; in other words, the serious business of *Halacha*[1] is more concerned with the right and proper use or observance of the *Shema* than in safeguarding this truth by definitive dogma. In a striking way the very structure and content of the *Shema* illustrates this preference of Judaism for fixing its belief by the experience and practice of religion. The *Shema* as an essential part of Jewish worship not only commits the worshipper to an acknowledgement of God but leads on directly to the glad acceptance of his sovereignty in the observance of *Mitzvot* (statutes and commandments) and diligent study of Torah. While there is no direct statement of God's sovereignty in the *Shema*, significantly enough the first sentence of the *Shema* in the Orthodox prayer book is followed by a doxology that extols God's sovereignty:

'Blessed be His name, whose glorious Kingdom is forever and ever.'

The idea that faith entails commitment to God's sovereignty is not exactly alien to the way that the New

---

[1] *Halacha* etymologically is derived from the verb 'to walk'. It is a technical term referring to the precise rabbinical directions for obligatory religious observances. *Halacha* plots the right path that every Jew should take.

138

Testament views belief in Jesus as Lord. What is, however, very strange to Christians and particularly to those within the Protestant tradition is the way in which the scriptural passages that comprise the *Shema* link this commitment to precise and definite observances. Dr Israel Abrahams, commenting on the content of the *Shema*, pithily sums it up[1]:

The words embodying the basic dogma and duty of Judaism, regarded as the quintessence of the Law, were to be constantly in the Israelite's memory, and to be visibly written before his eyes. They were to be impressed on the young . . . , to be recited in worship morning and evening, and the Law of which they formed the epitome was to be the subject of conversation and study at all times. They were to be a sign upon the hand and frontlets between the eyes—a precept which received literal fulfilment in the wearing of *tephillin* (phylacteries). They were also to be inscribed on the door-posts—an ordinance which gave rise to the *mezuzah* (lit. *door-post*, and thence the glass, wood, or metal case containing the first two paragraphs of the Shema: Deut. 6.4-9; 11.13-21). . . . The third paragraph of the Shema (Num. 15.37-41) ordains the wearing of *fringes* [which] were to act as a reminder to hold the Law in constant remembrance and thus they are similar in purpose with the *tephillin* and *mezuzah*, outward expressions of an inward thought.

This very brief commentary on the text of the *Shema* serves to illustrate how the whole rabbinic religion is both an extension of the *Shema* and at the same time a most faithful development of the pattern of religion evident in the text from the Pentateuch that comprises the *Shema*.

[1] *Annotated Edition of the Authorised Daily Prayer Book* (Eyre and Spottiswoode, London, 1914), Introduction, pp. liii-liv.

The point of supreme importance is to recognize that the whole pattern of rabbinic religion is not only a true development of an essential aspect of Old Testament religion (which insists, in the words Claude Montefiore, that 'feeling alone will not suffice; we need also will; and will alone will not suffice; it must be translated into deed'), but that in its totality is a massive demonstration of a whole people's experience and commitment to God. Suddenly the great detail of rabbinic religion in its meticulous observance of *Mitzvot* and devoted attention to the study of Torah becomes a harmonious whole. It is almost as if the specific concrete actions demanded in the practice of Judaism and so devotedly observed by a whole people are not merely individual precious stones but more significantly part of a magnificent mosaic whose complex pattern spells out only one word—GOD.

Admittedly this is a different reading of rabbinic religion from that prevalent in the Christian tradition. The tragedy with so much Christian evaluation of Judaism is that it fastened its total attention on a particular point of abuse and failure and naively thought that this was a true reading of the main significance of Judaism. It is all too easy to point out that the recitation of the *Shema* and literal observance of its demands in a *mezuza* on a doorpost, phylacteries on hands and forehead and fringes on clothes can be a meaningless ritual—it can. The rabbis were not only aware of this but even suggested how it might be avoided. *Keriat Shema*, that is the recitation of the *Shema*, needs to be accompanied by *Kavana*, the rabbis' term for attention of mind and direction of heart (cf. *Anthology*, pp. 273-4). Moreover, the rabbis realized that even this specific injunction about the necessary

140

direction of heart could not guarantee the effective fulfilment of the *Shema* (or any other religious observance);
but such possible and actual abuse does not destroy the
underlying motif and overall purpose to which the Jewish
fidelity in such details as *mezuza*, phylacteries and fringes
is a testimony—a whole people's commitment to the one
true and living God.

Undoubtedly there are many Christians who have
never heard of the rabbinic term *Shema* or are not particularly conscious of the Jewish hold upon monotheism:
but there would be few Christians who do not in some way
associate the Law with Judaism or who have not at some
time heard its Hebrew title Torah. Unfortunately it is
also true that at no other point in the Christian image of
Judaism have we so misunderstood and caricatured a
Jewish concept as is the case with Torah. This applies both
to the usual term 'Law' that we use for Torah as well as
to our whole conception of the scope, place, and use of
Torah. For us the Law as practised in Judaism has become
almost synonymous with 'legalism', 'externalism' and the
idea that it was a most 'burdensome' load. This, as we
have already noted in a previous chapter, is admittedly a
point of failure due to the misuse of Torah but it is very
far from its dominant concept and practice in Judaism.
Torah for the rabbis did include the idea of our English
term Law but we need to add several other words such
as 'teaching', 'instruction', 'direction', 'revelation' and
'Bible' if we are to approach the great richness and depth
of the Hebrew term Torah. It will at once be seen that
this is an inclusive concept and indeed the rabbis' glory in
the great expanse of the Torah. The Pesikta Rab Kahana
(*Anthology*, p. 167) expresses this thought:

And as the wilderness has no limit, so the words of the Law have no limit, as is said, 'The measure thereof is larger than the earth and broader than the sea' (Job 11.9).

The rabbis maintained that there was sufficient teaching in the Torah to satisfy all the intellectual needs of the Jewish community. Ingeniously enough this was seen as a reason why the Torah did not begin with the strictly legal section of the twelfth chapter of Exodus but with an account of creation and the origin of man so that it might reveal 'the whole mysteries of God's working in this world'.

While the Pentateuch takes precedence over the other two sections of the Old Testament, the Prophets and the Writings, these are not altogether excluded from the Torah as is indicated in a passage from the Midrash on Psalm 78 (*Anthology*, p. 159):

Let not a man say, the Psalms are not Torah; they are Torah, and the Prophets too are Torah, and the riddles and the parables are also Torah.

To this we must add the rabbinic extension of the Torah in Talmud and Midrash; and even this is not the limit of Torah, for rabbinical teaching that is soaked in Talmud and Midrash becomes in a loose way also a part of Torah. Perhaps there is an equivalent in the Evangelical tradition where it used to be not uncommon to ask the preacher 'to preach the Word' or to thank him afterwards for faithfully 'giving the Word'.

It will be readily seen that the possession of the Torah so manifold in its teaching was for the rabbis hardly a burdensome load that an austere deity had placed upon them but rather 'a pearl of great price', a treasure of immeasurable worth. The rabbis were even a little self-conscious about the fact that God should have given the Torah to Israel rather than to any other nation. Indeed that was the reason why it was given in the wilderness, a kind of no-man's land, rather than in the land particularly designated for Israel. The Mekhilta (*Anthology*, p. 166) underlines this idea.

The Law was given in the wilderness and in fire and in water. As these three are free to all the inhabitants of the world, so are the words of the Law free to all the inhabitants of the world.

The rabbis seem to suggest that all the nations started on an equal footing; what distinguishes Israel is their glad acceptance of the great treasure of Torah (cf. *Anthology*, p. 81).

The rabbis remembered that their forebears had had other valuable possessions such as the Temple, the Sacrifices, the Holy Land, yet although only the Torah remained it was of such value that it was by itself a sufficient substitute for all that had been so tragically lost. All the gifts of God to Israel were tokens of his favour and purpose for them, following upon their glad acceptance of the Torah. The fact that they continued to possess the Torah in exile was a sure guarantee that their special relationship to God had not been brought to an abrupt end (cf. *Anthology*, p. 116).

Not surprisingly, the rabbis loved to dwell on the beauty of this great treasure. Their thought at times does rather concentrate on the pride of possession, yet they realized that the Torah was a thing of no ordinary beauty, it was not an external possession that merely enhanced the out-

143

✓

ward appearance of Israel, it rather affected the inner beauty of character that prepared Israel for the world to come (cf. *Anthology*, p. 118).

The rabbis further qualified their pride of possession of the Torah by their immense sense of responsibility, in two directions. First, they were aware that such a weighty treasure as the Torah—though this is far from any idea of its being 'burdensome'—carried with it a correspondingly heavy responsibility to fulfil and keep it (cf. *Anthology*, p. 177). Secondly, the rabbis accepted a universal responsibility for bearing witness to the truth of the Torah to all nations. This was not the same as an all-out effort to proselytize among the nations by bringing members of other nations and religions to accept the Torah, but rather the intention of allowing the light of the Torah to reach out into the world among other nations and religions.

Out of Zion shall go forth the Law and the word of the Lord from Jerusalem (Isa. 11.3).

Just as the rabbis delighted in extolling the beauty of the Torah, so similarly they did not tire in praising its great practical value. They emphasized this in a number of ways and in particular by likening the Torah to the basic commodities of life such as water, wine, honey, oil and milk, suggesting that just as these commodities play a part in maintaining life and well-being, so too does the Torah.

It is from this vantage point of the great store that the rabbis set by the Torah that we can best understand their determination to keep and preserve it at all costs. The fence that the rabbis built around the Torah was not, as is so often supposed, a niggardly attention to the trivialities of the Torah (though at times they could descend to this) but rather a carefully thought-out determination to maintain its essential wholeness and unity. The Torah was God's gift to Israel, it was a complete gift sufficient as we have seen for all the contingencies of life, that was its glory. To pick and choose between the ceremonial and moral aspects, between the commandments that appeal and make sense and those that may be repugnant and whose reason is hidden from us, is to jeopardize not only the totality of the Torah but its whole authority. The rabbis upheld this concept of the totality and invulnerability of the Torah in many ways. In particular we may mention three.

The first is by their refusal to distinguish between secular and sacred aspects of the Torah. In their view religion was either all or nothing; and as they were profoundly religious, no aspect of life was outside the range of the Torah. Secondly, by their belief in *Torah min hashamayim* (that is, the Torah from heaven) the rabbis refused to recognize any differentiation between oral and written or ceremonial and moral elements in the Torah. All was part of the one complete and perfect Torah given at Sinai to Moses. Thirdly, the rabbis devised a subtle distinction between *Hukim* and *Mishpatim*—difficult terms to translate, perhaps the best rendering would be 'statutes' and 'judgements'. The purpose of this distinction was to recognize that there were certain injunctions of the Torah for which no reasonable explanation could be put forward, while in other instances the reason was self-evident. Quite unashamedly the rabbis maintain that the purpose behind the inexplicable *Hukim* was that God demanded blind obedience to the Torah and not merely the acceptance of certain injunctions that appealed to one's reason. The rabbis, however, did make the small concession that while they did not know the reason for the *Hukim*, Moses, to whom they were first entrusted, did, and so would they in the age to come. This sort of reasoning is quite unpalatable to us, and indeed to many Jews of today, and not least to many Jews in Israel where the demands of Torah are evident in the daily life of the country. We are confronted here with one of the most difficult aspects of the rabbinic concept of Torah, which is at the nerve centre of the contemporary crisis within Orthodoxy.[1]

Viewed from the historical perspective the rabbinic fence about the Torah was a most ingenious operation to maintain its relevance. Not only does it make sense because it was eminently suited for the situation, but it was also highly successful in preserving the Jewish religion and people as perhaps nothing else could have done. The modern crisis in Judaism arises from the sheer fact that the situation for which the fence was created is fast dis-

---

[1] This is well illustrated in the conflict between the former Chief Rabbi of Great Britain and Rabbi Louis Jacobs. The Chief Rabbi in his statement recorded in the *Jewish Chronicle* of 8 May 1964 emphasized that the controversy was on the fundamental issue of the invulnerability of the Torah in its entirety. He explains: 'The Torah, including the written and oral Law, is the very basis of Jewish existence. Once undermined, as our historical experience has proved, Jewish life and tradition weakens and withers and the way is open for the disappearance of the Jewish identity. . . . Dr Jacobs repeats the well-worn thesis that parts of the Torah are not Divine but are man-made, and maintains that reason alone should be the final judge as to what portion of the Torah may be selected as Divine. . . . If this were all that Dr Jacobs teaches and preaches, it would be incongruous for him to occupy the pulpit of an Orthodox synagogue.'

appearing. Western emancipated Jews do not feel that their Judaism can be safeguarded by being sheltered from the non-Jewish environment in which they 'live and move and have their being'. The Israeli Jews living once more in a sovereign and majority Jewish state are questioning the adequacy of a particular view and application of Torah that was for the most part worked out in a minority context. For this and other reasons there are disturbing voices within Judaism today who are asking whether the traditional fence with its particular application to Torah is still viable.

We shall need to return to this crisis within Judaism in our closing chapter. For the present it may be instructive to know that Christianity is facing a similar crisis in attempting to work out a meaningful and contemporary Christology. Judaism and Christianity have rightly refused superficial attempts to reduce their most fundamental concepts, that of Torah and the person and work of Jesus Christ. In many ways there is a real parallel in the centrality and significance of these two affirmations in the two religions. For both religions these focal points constitute the absolute and manifested will of God. There are many further parallels between these two central convictions, and this is particularly evident in the way in which the rabbis develop and extend—even personify— their concept of the Torah.

Just as the New Testament claims that all wisdom is summed up in Jesus, so the rabbis apply all the available Old Testament wisdom terminology to the Torah. Like the Logos in the prologue of St John's Gospel and the personification of wisdom in the eighth chapter of Proverbs, the Torah reflects the skill and wisdom by which

God created the world, and is thus by its very nature pre- and supra-mundane. Like the Logos, the Torah is particularly near to God, and the rabbis even go so far as to say that when God gave the Torah to Israel he was in a measure giving himself, for he cannot be altogether separated from his Torah (cf. *Anthology*, p. 271).

This parallel is even further extended in that the annunciation of the Torah at Sinai and the incarnation at Bethlehem are both seen as world-shaking events accompanied by the presence of angels. Yet we need to be cautious about making too much of such outward similarities which may only give a semblance of likeness rather than indicate a significant approximation in the two focal points in Judaism and Christianity. The rabbis' personification of the Torah and such related ideas never reach the point of dogma in Judaism. A lofty concept of Torah was undoubtedly of real importance to the rabbis yet their emphasis was primarily upon study and fulfilment. Sometimes their language might indicate that the mere possession of the text of Torah was sufficient but this is due more to their particular indulgence in hyperbole than to their lack of emphasis upon the study and doing of the Torah. Yet with all their insistence upon the excellence of study and the massive way in which they put this ideal into practice, the rabbis did not neglect the prime importance of motive and concentration in every activity applied to the Torah.

The rabbis had two distinctive words, *Lishma* and *Kavana*, to describe their idea of motive and concentration. The Torah must be studied for its own sake. There are rewards that follow upon the study of Torah but the rabbis are convinced that the Torah itself is its own

148

reward. In the Mishna (*Anthology*, p. 127) we read of Rabbi Johanan ben Zakkai who said:

> If thou hast learned much Torah, take not credit for thyself, for thereunto wast thou created. R. Jose said: 'Let all thy deeds be done for the sake of Heaven.'

Similarly the rabbis emphasized the compelling need for proper concentration of mind and direction of heart. This in their own language is their insistence on the need of *Kavana* in the basic study of Torah, which is none other than the recitation of the *Shema*. The worshipper and the student alike 'must pause, direct his heart to God with awe and fear . . . every single word with heartfelt sincerity' (*Anthology*, p. 273)—that is, *Kavana*!

Mitzvot (or its singular *Mitzva*), a difficult term to interpret that might perhaps be translated as 'statutes' and 'commandments', is the last of the rabbinic concepts that we are able to consider in our present study. We can hardly separate the idea of *Mitzvot* from Torah, as it is essentially part and parcel of the larger concept of Torah. In one sense it is yet another example of the rabbinic emphasis on the experience and practice of religion that we have already noted. The rabbis do not give us any careful differentiation between Torah and *Mitzvot*; indeed often the terms are interchangeable. We might think that the Torah belongs to the realm of study, and *Mitzvot* to fulfilment and doing, then surprisingly enough we are confronted by the injunction to fulfil and carry out Torah and to study *Mitzvot*. The whole idea of *Mitzva* represents the successful way in which the rabbis translated the perfect will of God for a whole community into concrete acts that could be carried out at every turn of the 'daily round, the common task'. The doing of *Mitzvot* was certainly obligatory, yet for the rabbis it was an occasion of spontaneous joy. They could not conceive of a greater benefit than was inherent in the sheer keeping, doing and fulfilling of statutes, commandments and ordinances. It is from this angle that we shall be able to understand how very differently the rabbis view the multiplication of *Mitzvot*.

To us the very fact that the Torah was comprised of six hundred and thirteen commandments is a most disconcerting fact. How could such numerous obligations not be essentially burdensome? The rabbis viewed this quite differently. Beside the fact that many of the six hundred and thirteen commandments were altogether obsolete we do not hear of any one rabbi who set out to keep the whole number; indeed, when pressed, the rabbis were quite able to reduce the commandments to one single principle, as is evident from an oft-repeated quotation from the Babylonian Talmud (*Anthology*, p. 199):

R. Simlai said: 'Six hundred and thirteen commandments were given to Moses, 365 negative commandments, answering to the number of the days of the year, and 248 positive commandments, answering to the number of a man's members. Then David came and reduced them to eleven [eleven commandments are found in Psalm 15]. Then came Isaiah, and reduced them to six [as one may count in Isa. 33.15]. Then came Micah, and reduced them to three [as is seen in the great saying of Micah 6.8]. Then Isaiah came again, and reduced them to two, as is said, "Keep ye judgement and righteousness." Then came Amos, and reduced them to one, as it is said, "Seek ye me and live." Or one may say, then came Habakkuk (2.4), and reduced them to one, as is said, "The righteous shall live by his faith." '

The Message of Judaism

The rabbis' insistence on the significance of all the commandments was to ensure that none should be excluded or treated as unimportant. If any kind of differentiation was allowed would this not be the thin end of the wedge that could all too easily lead to a wholesale overthrow of the Torah (cf. *Anthology*, p. 157)? The rabbis extended this line of thought by emphasizing the great value of fulfilling one commandment perfectly, and perfection for the rabbis was not achieved unless the doing of a *Mitzva* was accompanied with joy (cf. *Anthology*, pp. 202-3). The great number of *Mitzvot*, far from being burdensome to the rabbis, emphasized God's goodness in thus multiplying Israel's opportunity to grow in virtue. It was a matter for rejoicing that the multiplication of the *Mitzvot* assured every Israelite that there was no situation in which a commandment could not be fulfilled. This idea is even further extended in the rabbinic concept of *Mitzva she-Kaha*, that is 'the commandment with regard to forgetfulness.' In this idea we see the spontaneous joy that some of the rabbis experienced when they were allowed to fulfil an extra *Mitzva* which cannot be accomplished at any time but only inadvertently (cf. *Anthology*, p. 192).

If after all this we are still unconvinced that Torah and *Mitzvot* were a genuine source of joy in Judaism, then perhaps we should forget all theorization about this and seek an occasion to be present at the annual feast of *Simhat Torah* (the Joy of the Torah) particularly as this is celebrated in the infectious atmosphere of almost wild enthusiasm in Israel today. But there is no need to wait for an annual celebration or to travel to Israel. The joy of Torah and *Mitzvot* may also be experienced, if perhaps in a somewhat more restrained atmosphere, in the way that every orthodox Jewish family welcomes the Sabbath, week in and week out, in their family meal on *Erev Shabbat* (eve of the Sabbath, that is Friday evening).

It must be admitted that we have been representing the rabbinic concepts of Torah and *Mitzvot* at their ideal level, but we can hardly expect to draw out the great value that these truths in Judaism have for us as Christians unless we allow them to confront us in their great strength and ideal expression.

The rabbis, like other religious leaders, were fully conscious of how short their people often fell of this ideal. Their great achievement lay in the impressive extent to which the Torah not only became the accepted manifestation of God's will for Israel but also was realized as the understood and practised civic, moral and religious standard of a whole people. The refusal of the rabbis to distinguish between secular and sacred aspects of the Torah achieved in the practice of Judaism a rare integration and wholeness that knew nothing of our separation into water-tight compartments of religion and the rest of life.

It was this total implication of Torah for the whole of life and the entire community, coupled with the fundamental belief that the Torah is the expressed and perfect will of God, that enabled the rabbis to assert that where this Torah was practised there the Kingdom of God, or rather God's Kingly Rule, was operative and realized. They knew that all too often God's Kingly Rule was thwarted in the community of Israel, but they rejoiced in any and every concrete act in which the will of God in Torah was actualized by the practice of *Mitzvot* in the life of the individual and community. It was this association of *Mitzva* with the will of God in Torah brilliantly translated into action that gave its great worth to every good deed accomplished by a Jew. The great strength of *Mitzvot* is that they provide for every Jew a daily opportunity to translate his religion into concrete and worthwhile deeds.

The rabbis, like other religious teachers and leaders, made their mistakes, had their serious blind spots, do not possess all the clues for the needs of religion in the twentieth century, yet at many points they are significantly instructive for us moderns. What is more, just as Christianity believes that it has maintained 'the faith once delivered to the saints', so Judaism equally claims that it has faithfully kept the practice of religion as first entrusted to Moses in the giving of the Torah and as centred, from that day to the present, in God's declared will in the Torah expounded by the rabbis in Talmud and Midrash observed and continued in contemporary Judaism.

If we can attentively hear the rabbis in their massive affirmation of God in the *Shema*, in their abiding conviction of God's nearness in the *Shechina*, in their integrated concept of Torah for all life and the entire community, in their whole-hearted insistence on and practice of goodness in *Mitzvot*, we shall begin to understand how much we have missed in by-passing Judaism in the past and how great the riches that are open to us when we are prepared to learn from the religion symbolized by the Torah. In the beautiful words of the Midrash Exodus Rabba XVII.2 (Soncino edition, p. 212):

We know the power of the Torah, therefore we will not budge from God and His Torah, as it says: 'Under its shadow I delighted to sit, and its fruit was sweet to my taste.'

153

5

Christians and Jews

>>>◆<<<

At this point *all* Judaeo-Christian dialogue ends in the ancient petition of the Pater Noster: 'Thy kingdom come to us,' just as the New Testament, conscious of its own unfulfilment, with its concluding words, utters the prayer, 'Amen. Come, Lord Jesus!' And the Kaddish prayer of the Jew concludes with the same petition for fulfilment, of which no one knows whether it may come tomorrow, for the messianic kingdom which, in spite of all deceptions and disappointments, always is awaited in the day to come with the same fervor—morning, afternoon, and evening of every day of this aeon: 'May he bring his kingdom to dominion within your lifetime and within your days and within the lifetime of the whole house of Israel—shortly, within a brief time.'[1] *Hans Joachim Schoeps*

If Christians and Jews are also human—and let us hope that they are—they will certainly wish to have human communication. Perhaps the land of Israel is the place where such communication may be established sooner and with a better chance of success than elsewhere. *R. J. Zwi Werblowsky*

FROM what has already been said in the foregoing pages, it is obvious that a proper renovation of the Christian-

[1] *The Jewish-Christian Argument*, Eng. trans. by D. E. Green (Holt, Rinehart and Winston, New York, 1963), p. 172.

Christians and Jews

Jewish relationship is no light or easy matter. It is not a case of mere adjustment to the modern situation, or a general overhaul of 'our method of approach' which might be described as a 'wash and brush-up'. Rather what is involved is in every sense as complex and intricate an operation as is envisaged when a surgeon attempts to effect a genuine 'face-lift' after a serious and disfiguring accident. So far we have been primarily concerned with the all-important pre-operational 'scrub-up', and we have yet two further items that belong to this preparation before we can turn our attention to the more exciting task of reconstructing the new face.

1. We have made several allusions, particularly in chapters 2 and 3, to the traditional Christian apologetics to the Jews as they crystallized in the historic disputations. Of this considerable body of literature the second-century work the *Dialogue of Justin Martyr with Trypho* is, as we have noted, of crucial importance because it ably sums up the Christian argument in the post-apostolic period and delineates the pattern of subsequent disputations. In size it approximates the four Gospels. The bulk of its contents is taken up with detailed interpretations of specific Old Testament passages by which Justin attempts to prove that Jesus and none other was the Messiah that the Old Testament predicted. While his Jewish opponent Trypho is very much 'a man of straw', the strong Jewish rejoinders to this major Christian thrust are apparent in Trypho's main reply that many Old Testament predictions of the Messiah are not fulfilled by Jesus' Messianic role. Justin's reply to this is twofold. Either he disputes the Jewish interpretation or even the actual text of a particularly awkward Old Testament passage, or he main-

155

tains that this or that Old Testament promise or prediction (such as the promised universal peace of Isaiah 11) will only be fulfilled by the second coming of Jesus.

We have already noted in the second chapter that one cannot use the Old Testament as 'decisive proof texts'. Even a cursory study of Justin's *Dialogue* demonstrates how inevitably such argument led to a deadlock. At the same time it is only fair that we should note that there are already (admittedly very faint!) traces in Justin's *Dialogue* (cf. 39.7 and 88) that both the Christian and Jewish disputants were aware of the inadequacy of their argument from the Old Testament to furnish them with convincing proof. This is also obliquely discernible in many of the subsequent disputations by the fact that so often the Christian disputant has to resort to a miracle or to rely upon special privileges available to him from his exalted patronage. The position is in no way improved by the fact that we have in the past tended to evaluate the Jewish answers from disputations recorded by Christians. At best the Jewish answers have been somewhat soft-pedalled and at worst they have been what Christians suppose the Jews should have answered rather than genuine Jewish replies. Fortunately it is not necessary to rely on the Christian disputations, for there have also been Jewish scholars who have taken to the offensive. The most comprehensive Jewish answer is in a sixteenth-century work by Rabbi Isaac of Troki known as the *Chizzuk Emunah* (the strengthening of faith). It should be added that this work misrepresents the Christian point of view just as much as the Christian disputations tended to do with the Jewish viewpoint. Another full-scale Jewish reply to the historic Christian argument is that by Paul

Goodman under the title of *The Synagogue and the Church*,[1] 'Being a Contribution to the Apologetics of Judaism'. It reflects a rather negative orthodox attitude to Christianity, but it nonetheless gives a recent and detailed refutation of the traditional Christian argument from the Old Testament. Although the *Dialogue* was written in the second century and *The Synagogue and the Church* in the first decade of the twentieth century, the chapter in this work on 'Messianic Prophecies' can be placed alongside the main content of the *Dialogue*. They deal with the same matter—is it any wonder that both Christians and Jews feel that the arguments have been repeated *ad nauseam*? Significantly Professor Moule detected how very little use our New Testament writers make of an obvious Old Testament passage greatly employed in subsequent Christian disputations—Isaiah 53. Professor Moule pertinently remarks:

One can only surmise that it had somehow been vitiated for this purpose—that it had already been spoiled or blunted as an argument directed to the Jews, by some circumstances no longer clearly discernible to us.[2]

Is this not what is true of the whole pattern of traditional argument from Old Testament proof texts? There may well be Christian readers who would object to this on the grounds that it is a form of argument greatly employed in the New Testament, but to what extent is this true? Recent New Testament studies, particularly in St John's Gospel, are revealing other types of debate with the Jews

[1] *The Synagogue and the Church* (Routledge, London, 1908).
[2] *The Birth of the New Testament* (A. & C. Black, London, 1962), p. 82.

apart from the dominant pattern in St Matthew. We have noted in chapter 3 how this debate centred in live theological issues that were extended and intensified up to the period of separation in the early second century. It is at least worthwhile to ask whether the historic pattern of the Christian disputations does not owe more to the period after the separation, when the debate with the Synagogue was virtually closed and what had been a genuine dialogue gave way to a continuous but monotonous monologue, than to the New Testament itself. One further and most important fact is that since the debate in the New Testament period there has come into being a Jewish literature parallel to the New Testament. This literature also claims to be an interpretation and continuation of the Old Testament, and that in itself, quite apart from all else that has happened since then in the Christian-Jewish relationship, changes the situation from what it was in New Testament times.

2. So far we have avoided direct reference to the modern Christian missionary enterprise among Jews that arose directly out of the emergence of the modern missionary movement in the eighteenth century. There are Catholic organizations that are more directly related to the mediaeval Christian missionary effort but were also rejuvenated in the wake of the great modern missionary upsurge. Dr Parkes, who has been and remains an outspoken critic of the very existence of 'Jewish Missions', makes a very simple and yet moving commendation of Christian Missions in general. He writes:

The missionary activity of the Christian Church is something unique. When all possible criticism has been levelled at it, there remains an ineffaceable deposit of nobility and service which is a permanent part of the history of humanity.[1]

This the present writer believes is also applicable to the history of Christian missions to Jews. Much detail could be added on the credit side in an honest appraisal of Jewish missions but it is perhaps sufficient to mention that among the most dedicated Christian stalwarts against anti-semitism have been those who themselves have been involved in Christian missions to Jews. It is also true that some of the most noted Christian Hebraists were led to their study and appreciation of Jewry and Judaism by their involvement in Jewish missions. The Jewish Publication Society in their recent production in a paperback of Herman Strack's monumental *Introduction to Talmud and Midrash* made this significant comment:

The German Protestant theologian and Orientalist Herman L. Strack was born in 1848 and died in 1924. From 1877 he was Professor of Old Testament exegesis and Semitic language at the University of Berlin. He was the foremost Christian authority of his day on Talmudic and rabbinic literature, having studied rabbinics under Moritz Steinschneider. Although Professor Strack was active in the conversionary Institutum Judaicum, he was vigorous in his defence of Jews and Judaism against resurgent German anti-Semitism.

The truth of this and much more that could be added should not however blind us to the serious criticisms that have been levelled from within the Christian tradition itself against the particular structure and method of operation of the missionary societies. Heinz Leuner in a

[1] *Jewry and Jesus of Nazareth* (joint pamphlet with Maurice Eisendrath, The Parkes Library, Royston, Herts, 1964), pp. 18-19.

most pertinent article 'From Mission to Dialog[1]' has competently collated together such criticisms. These are directed against the calibre and qualifications of missionary personnel, strategy, methods and literature and not least the missions' attitude to Judaism and the Jewish convert.

Even though it is true that many societies have now put their house in order, it is most regrettably not true of all. Yet even if all the societies were totally cleared from the above abuses we should still have to face the far more radical question of a new confrontation which among many other factors, presupposes a very different relationship between the two faiths from that which lies at the back of the traditional missionary approach. At the same time it is most likely that if the missionary societies honestly followed through the implications of criticisms referred to above it would in all probability lead them on into the direction of the new confrontation here suggested. Is it not possible that what is holding the missionary societies back is an understandable fear that if the traditional ways are given up then perhaps all is lost? Certainly it is not easy to move from the idea of individual conversions to that of genuine communal confrontation—but it seems that it is nothing less that we are being called to do.

Perhaps the first point that should be made in any attempt to delineate a tentative outline of the new relationship is to recognize that 'Now we see only puzzling reflections in a mirror' (I Cor. 13.12, NEB). No one can afford, and least of all the present writer, to be dogmatic in this area, for we are at present, both Christians and Jews, only feeling our way, we are very much in a diffi-

[1] *The Lutheran World*, October 1963, cf. particularly pp. 391-3.

cult yet exciting explorative stage. The four following suggestions are offered by an explorer who has not yet arrived.

(a) It will involve us as members of the Christian Church in a full and total recognition of and repentance for all that we have discovered has been wrong in our attitude to and treatment of Jewry and Judaism. It is certainly true that the Church has already made a good beginning in this direction,[1] but unfortunately we have tended to *minimize* the extent of our involvement in anti-semitism and to stop short of the religious roots of anti-Judaism. To express this in other words is to recognize that we have to follow through to the bitter end the evil effect that the two primary anti-Jewish accusations— that 'the Jews' are guilty of deicide and that Judaism is decadent—have had on Christian teaching and the Church's attitude to Jewry and Judaism. Nothing less than a total reversal of these false propositions can possibly prepare the way for a new and creative confrontation.

(b) If it is true that 'the Jews' are not guilty of deicide and that Judaism as it has been classically expressed by rabbinic orthodoxy is the practice of an ethnico-religious people who have never been displaced as God's People, then it is no longer possible for Christians to maintain that they and their religion are under God's curse. To express this in other words is to acknowledge, as the

[1] See Appendix I for the Roman Catholic declaration in the Vatican Ecumenical Council II and for a recent statement by the Archbishop of Canterbury. The World Council of Churches has issued several statements which have in the main been limited to a repudiation of anti-semitism. A brief survey of these statements is given in an article on the 'Work of the Committee on the Church and the Jewish People', by the Rev. Anker Gjerding (*Lutheran World*, October 1963).

great rabbinic concept of *Shechina* has consistently maintained, that God has not withdrawn his presence from them. It is to assert with St Paul that 'God has not rejected the people which he acknowledged of old as his own' that 'God's choice stands' for 'theirs is the splendour of the divine presence' (Rom. 11.1, 28; 9.4, NEB). This is in no sense a pious platitude or a shallow overture of friendship towards Jews, for if we follow through this conviction it has most far-reaching results and in particular we may enumerate two. (i) As we have noted in chapter 4, the recognition of God's presence in Judaism requires from us the humble approach that is prepared to listen and learn from what Judaism has to say to us in our understanding of God and his will for us and the world. (ii) We cannot simply resume this 'listening and learning' in the twentieth century as though our deafness to God's voice in Judaism for so long has had no effect in the way we have understood and interpreted our faith. To coin a new expression we need to trace the effect that this *non-Judaism* (which arose out of the Church's anti-Judaism) has had on the development of Christian doctrine. We have already hinted in our discussion on God's oneness how perilously near the Christian doctrine of the Trinity at times approaches to that of 'tritheism'. Would this have happened if the Church had been more aware of the Jewish declaration of the one God? We need to go on and ask serious questions about the particular formulation of our Christology. Would the Church have remained more true to the New Testament emphasis that always relates our Lord to God? What of some extreme devotion to our Lord that in some instances developed into what has been termed 'Jesus worship' and speaks of him as a separate

162

God? Our inquiry here will also lead us to examine the Catholic devotion to Mary, the mother of Jesus, which at times approaches dangerously near to exalting her to the status of a goddess. Further we shall need to ask what effect the Christian minimizing of the Jewish concept of Torah has had on the Christian observance of an accepted standard of behaviour particularly as this applies to the community. Is it an accident or coincidence that it is around these two questions of 'our image of God' and an acceptable authoritative 'standard of morality' that Christians today are being challenged to do their most serious re-thinking?

(c) Without minimizing any of the above implications we cannot pretend that the Christian-Jewish alienation is totally explained by the foregoing considerations. It is not. Granted that the Jewish attitude to Jesus is often a result of the Christian mistreatment of Jews and that much of the Jewish aversion to Christian doctrine is the result of the Church's unfaithfulness to her Jewish heritage there is at a deep level in the relationship of the two faiths a 'theological tension' that arises directly out of the differing emphasis in the religion of Torah and that of the Incarnation. This at first centred around the question of the acceptance of Jesus as the Messiah, but quickly developed into a more complex theological controversy over the universalistic implications of the Christian Gospel and the ethnic emphasis on the complete observance of the Torah. It is at this point that Judaism will need to share in the 'face-lift'. It will involve Judaism, as we have already indicated at the close of chapter 3, in a radical reappraisal of Jesus. Further, Judaism will need to face the whys and wherefores of her religious and ethnic

163

rigidity. This issue is at the heart of the contemporary crisis in Judaism, as this is evident both in the conflict in Britain concerning Rabbi Louis Jacobs and in the fierce controversy between Orthodoxy and Jewish deviationist groups (ancient and modern) in Israel. Another relevant issue is whether Judaism has not in some sense failed to be true to the universalistic implications inherent in her election. In other words, is Judaism fulfilling her mission to the world or has this to a large measure been taken over by Christianity? It is with considerable diffidence that these suggestions are being put forward; such things need to be said by Jews and happily to some measure they are being said by Jews. We have already at the close of chapter 3 drawn attention to Rabbi Maurice Eisendrath's call for a new Jewish orientation to Jesus. This, together with some of the issues raised above, has been expressed by another Jewish scholar, Rabbi David Polish. Writing of the possibility of an ultimate Christian-Jewish reconciliation he remarks:

On the part of Judaism, this would involve a readiness to confront Christianity in terms of a new situation and a new relationship brought about by the emergence of the state of Israel. The relationship brought about by centuries of exile would no longer be valid, and while the memories of persecution could not be effaced, the recriminations would be silenced. This would also involve Judaism's recognition that covenantal relationships are not exclusive nor limited, and that Christianity, like Judaism, stands in a special but different relationship to God. Ever since the new Yishuv began, a special interest in Jesus has been manifested. This does not indicate, as some Christian theologians have wishfully stated, a turning towards Christianity. It does, however, show that in the free atmosphere of Israel, a new approach toward Jesus, removed from the realm of polemics or vituperation common to mediaeval Judaism, is taking place. It is to be expected that in the land where Jesus lived and from which the Christian message went forth, a deep interest should be stirred among Jews.[1]

(d) So far it might be possible for Christians and Jews to effect a renovation of their relationship, reaching out to each other as it were from a respectable distance, but further progress is hardly possible without entering into an intimate and costly dialogue. In other words, it is not merely a question of putting right what we discover to be wrong in our attitude to each other and our beliefs, but going on to explore if it is possible to hold and be faithful to what God has entrusted to each of us and yet move forwards towards a creative confrontation that may end in full integration and unity. Let us explore further. Granted that there exists the 'theological tension' referred to above we need to go on and ask, first, whether this tension was so fundamental that a separation between Church and Synagogue was inevitable, and, then, pressing our question even further, whether even if such a separation was at first inevitable the difference between Christianity and Judaism is of such a nature that there can never be a true integration and reconciliation in the future?

As to the first question, Travers Herford (one of the first Christian scholars to achieve an honest appraisal of Pharisaism) gives us his answer on which it is difficult to improve:

[1] *The Eternal Dissent* (Abelard-Schuman, London, New York and Toronto, 1961), p. 207.

The conflict between the Pharisees and Jesus has been, in its essence, a conflict between two types of religion, each valid on its own premises, and each having a right to exist, but such that neither could be assimilated to the other. The religion of the Pharisees was expressed in terms of Torah; its central feature was an Idea, an intellectual as well as a moral conception, by means of which it defined and represented the relation of the human soul to God. The religion of Jesus was not expressed in terms of Torah, and did not centre on an Idea. It was the outcome of his own immediate consciousness of God, apart from all forms of thought, apart from all traditional authority. Now the conflict between Judaism and Christianity was inevitable for much the same reason. . . .[1]

As to our second question we need to recognize that, however true it may be that the separation was at first inevitable, that does not necessarily mean that an ultimate integration and reconciliation is impossible. It must have seemed very revolutionary in the nineteen-twenties for a Christian scholar to suggest that the justification for the continued existence of Judaism was that it perpetuated a valid type of religion that was essentially different from Christianity. This was a necessary intermediary stage to the bolder hope here cherished. Dr Jacob Jocz, in a recent article on 'A Theology of Tension Resulting from the Juxtaposition of Church and Synagogue',[2] expounds in some detail the religious value of the 'theological tension' that exists between the Church and Synagogue. He explains:

Here Israel as a community, as a fellowship, as a family,

[1] *The Pharisees* (Allen and Unwin, 1924), p. 214.
[2] In two parts in *Judaica* (Zurich), June and September 1964. Quotation from p. 176.

166

questions the Church about her unity, about her fellowship, about her family cohesion: is the divided, splintered, broken body of Christ, the people of God? In the same special context, Israel with his prophetic zeal for social justice asks his opposite how she manages to reconcile the anguish of the nations with her messianic faith. But the Church too has some embarrassing questions to ask about Israel's repose in himself, his lack of missionary zeal, his rejection of the Messiah, his 'pre-occupation with mundane hopes'. On the arena of history Israel and Church thus face each other in a moral challenge.

Perhaps we may express this in another way by saying that Christians and Jews need each other, and only as they come together can they really discover what it is to be and to fulfil their high calling as the People of God. Is this any more than reaching out to St Paul's immense vision, in which he is able to believe that the God who is the 'Source, Guide, and Goal of all that is' (Rom. 11.36, NEB), has a purposed climax for what in the present may seem a permanent separation in the People of God? Dare we hope and work for anything less than this ultimate unity of the People of God?

It would be foolish to think that this ultimate goal is only 'around the corner'. It would be far nearer the truth to say that we are only just beginning 'to think about it'. It is nothing short of a miracle that at a time when the Church and Synagogue are reaching out to each other in a new and exciting way there should suddenly come into being a live situation (a *Sitz im Leben*) in which a true communal confrontation and dialogue on the lines that we have been discussing might more easily take place. This new opportunity is centred in the modern State of Israel.

This can be seen as a complete reversal of the historic Jewish-Christian relationship which, since the fourth century, has been that of a Christian majority usually supported by political sovereignty over and against a minority and politically dependent Jewish people. It is this pattern that the fact of Israel has reversed as far as the Christian Churches in that country are concerned. We are accustomed both in Africa and Asia to the new relationship that is created (and yet in a deeper sense has to be acknowledged and worked out) between a former colonial power and a newly independent State. This normal change has taken place between Israel and the former mandatory power of Great Britain. But in many ways Israel's ascent to modern independence is unusual, and this is particularly true of the religious involvement. The creation of the State was not merely the achievement of political independence from the mandatory power but also the re-embodiment of Judaism with her external vesture of the land of her origin and sustenance. Rabbi Yitzhak Ha' Cohen Kook, the first Chief Rabbi of Palestine, often pondered on this theme, maintaining that Judaism separated from her land was like a disembodied spirit. It is this union of land, people and religion, which had been severed for so long and now in Israel has once more achieved a visible unity, that gives the modern State its unique place in the Jewish world. It is this particular significance of Israel that has suddenly placed the Christian Churches (for the most part unprepared) in that State in a central and crucial position in the total relation of the Church and the Jewish people.

This new situation challenges the Christian Church to articulate her attitude and relationship both to the majority religion, that is, rabbinical Judaism, and to the context of the independent State in which the Church is located. As to the former the emergence of the State draws into a focal point the past relationship of the Church and the Jewish people and uncomfortably challenges us concerning it. It is as if the past Christian treatment of the Jewish people has suddenly been caught up and concentrated into the present relationship of Christians and Jews in Israel.

As far as a Christian answer about the modern State of Israel itself is concerned, it seems one of the ironies of history that at a time when the Church is trying desperately to move into a new relationship with the Jewish people her answers should be complicated by political overtones and the clear duty to remain sensitive to the Arab point of view. So far, the Latin Church has avoided any clear recognition of the State, and this very much marred the otherwise highly successful visit of the Pope in 1963. Individual Protestant Christians have proffered numerous answers. Some have even viewed the State as detailed fulfilment of prophecy, but this is often too forced and artificial ever to win general Christian agreement. Perhaps the best pointers for a fully worked out Christian answer have come from Mr Ellison and Dr Parkes. In a small monograph on *The State of Israel and the Interpretation of Prophecy*,[1] Mr Ellison maintains that the broad lines of prophecy indicate a definite association between the Jewish people and the Holy Land and that there is no statement in the scriptures to suggest that this link was severed by the emergence of the Christian Church. Dr Parkes in his published lecture on *The Con-*

[1] Prophecy Investigation Society, London, 1960.

169

tinuity of Jewish Life in the Middle East[1] convincingly argues for a continuing historic association of the Jewish people and the Holy Land. He has further reinforced this argument in his recent Brodetzky Lecture in which he maintained that the actual composition of the State today is largely that of Middle-Eastern Jews so that Israel is, in fact, as well as by right, a Middle-Eastern state. While at the present there is no generally accepted Christian answer, providing one is a task which the Church in Israel and ultimately the whole Church can hardly set aside.

David Polish, writing from the Jewish point of view, deepens and sharpens this issue:

Jewish Jerusalem as the capital of the Jewish state would not trouble the minds of some Christian statesmen and nations if the theological implications which its return to Jewish hands poses were not so evident. This and related problems are now confronting the best minds in Christendom. Extensive discussions in the area of Christianity's concern with the state of Israel can be found in a collection of essays, 'The Church and the Jewish People'. To be sure, the writers in this collection do not come to grips with the challenge which the Jewish restoration presents to Christian theology.[2]

If our reading of the Israeli situation is correct, namely, that the very existence of the State of Israel is a crucial reversal of the past and that it is this religio-political achievement that relates the other unchanged aspects of the past to the present, then the point which for theological reasons we have already seen to be the true and only possible starting place for a new relationship is also the precise point where the modern State impinges upon

[1] The Anglo-Israel Association, London, 1963.
[2] *The Eternal Dissent*, p. 203.

the Church in Israel. This is underlined by the frequent
mention of the Church's historic attitude to Jewry and
Judaism in the Israeli Press. Christians both within and
without the State are often bewildered why the presence
of such a small minority Christian Church (fifty thousand
of all denominations, of which forty-eight thousand are
Arab Christians, out of a total population of two and
three-quarter million of which two and a half million are
Jews) should call forth so much adverse comment. At the
time of Pope Paul's historic pilgrimage to the Holy Land,
Geoffrey Wigoder, a well known Israeli commentator on
Jewish affairs, wrote in the *Jerusalem Post* (3 January
1964) an article entitled 'The Church faces the Synagogue'. He writes:

What is certain is that the attitude of the Church initiated
or exacerbated anti-Semitism to a chronic extent. . . . The
patristic portrait of the Jew as perpetually betraying God and
ultimately abandoned by Him has informed Catholic dogma
to the present day and has sowed the seeds of modern anti-
Semitism. That is why the acceptance by the Ecumenical
Council of Cardinal Bea's document could be so significant.

But this is only one side of the deeply felt Jewish conviction in Israel about religion. Israeli Jews are also concerned about the condition of the major and established
religion. It may be true that the most vociferous Jewish
opinion comes from the non-religious Western Jews, well
represented in the League for the Prevention of Religious
Coercion, which is convinced that Orthodoxy is so out of
tune with the contemporary situation in Israel, that the
only solution is a complete separation of the Jewish religion from the Jewish State. This is a solution contrary to

the whole structure of Judaism, which has always maintained a unique link between religion, land, and people, but there is at a much deeper level a demand often coming from within Orthodoxy itself that religion should be made relevant to the Israel of today. The tragedy of the unhappy and often tense religious situation in Israel arises out of the inertia that is unfortunately true both of the Synagogue and Church. The more our eyes focus on the actual situation in Israel the more preposterous does the idea of an effective 'face-lift' between the two faiths in that area become. Yet the possibility is there, and for those who have eyes and ears there are some good portents in both communities. It is here possible to give only one or two illustrations. In Orthodoxy we can point to the serious interest and concern to interpret the Torah that is symbolized in all the effort centred in the Department for Torah Education and Culture of the World Zionist Organization in Jerusalem. Perhaps even more significant is the Orthodox Religious Kibbutz Movement. Michael Perlman of the Yavne Kibbutz, which has distinguished itself by building a beautiful Synagogue in contemporary style, writes:

The fabric of our life is reflected in our service to the Creator. We note with much concern the order of prayer customary in the cities and the towns in Israel. The services there do not attract the younger generation, generally speaking, for suitable aesthetic forms are not fostered; often even the Sephardi pronunciation is not introduced. We are concerned with questions of education and as such ask: How are we to ensure that our youth remain religious as they grow older? We seek to provide a suitable reply. We members of HaKibbutz HaDati do not claim that we have found the answers to all the questions that are troubling us. But we have recognized the problems. Future generations will pass judgement on the solutions we are developing, on the thought and the effort we have invested in beautifying our synagogue and our customs, in blending our worship within the framework of halutzic living, in harmonizing our prayer service with the revival of Judaism in its own land.[1]

This and many other factors indicate the genuine spiritual renewal that is taking place within Orthodoxy in Israel. But for all that the general image of Orthodoxy is still that of a complacent rigidity, and it seems that this rigidity is very much a legacy of the unhappy relationship with Christianity and that until this ancient enmity has been resolved there will be an essential blockage to a free flow of spiritual power and renewal. On the Continent of Europe there are good signs that this is being realized on the Jewish side, while at present there is a marked hesitancy on the part of religious Jews in Israel to move towards a genuine communal confrontation with the Christian Church. Dr Chaim Wardi, Counsellor on Christian Concerns to the Minister of Religious Affairs, in an article on 'The Christian Problem in Israel' (*Judaica*, June 1960) clearly recognizes the potential in Israel and a Jewish share in the responsibility for bringing about 'the renovation of the relationship between Judaism and Christianity'. Here and there one hears of the demand of certain *Sabras* (an Israeli-born Jew) for an explanation of Jesus and Christianity freed from the polemics of the past. However barely perceptible such and similar signs may be at present they have at least the vigour of eman-

[1] *The Religious Kibbutz Movement*, edited by Aryei Fishman (Zionist Organization, Jerusalem, 1957), pp. 66-67.

ating from the new and exciting present. If only the unhappy past could be dealt with and thus left behind there is every hope that religious Jewry in Israel would rise to the situation and move forward toward a creative spiritual confrontation.

Is it possible to see any signs of renewal and outreach on the lines discussed above in the small Christian Church in Israel today? Much can be said (and is being said) of the real failure of the Church in Israel to orient itself to the new situation, but there are also unmistakably some good portents. The Acts of the Apostles records (in ch. 15) an agreed statement issued by the Church in Jerusalem; the Church in Israel made history when for the first time in the modern era it also issued an agreed statement of all the sections of the Church (Roman Catholic, Greek Catholic, Orthodox, Anglican and Protestant) declaring their intention and activity in Israel today. The statement reads:

Israeli newspapers have, during recent years, published a number of accusations against Christians in Israel for an attitude designated as 'missionary' with a bad sense. These accusations have sometimes resulted from lack of information, sometimes seemed ill-intentioned, but were always painful to those who respect the liberty of conscience of others. We the undersigned affirm that our communities are not 'missionary' in a derogatory sense which some attach to this word.

We do not exploit the economic situation of an Israel citizen —his poverty, unemployment, inadequate housing or desire to emigrate—in order to induce conversion; because faith in our eyes is a free gift of God and a disinterested response on the part of man.

Nor do we take advantage, with the view to conversion, of a negative psychological attitude some Jews may feel towards

Israel, whether evidenced by bitterness or the desire to escape from their Jewishness; for we are convinced that a Jew who becomes a Christian still remains a member of his people, as he was from birth.

In our schools, hospitals, and other institutions our desire is to provide service in these fields. We do not exercise religious coercion in them.

Our positive aims are:

1. To help the members of our communities to be better Christians and better citizens.

2. To testify that Jesus is the source of truth and life for all mankind, by worship, in friendship towards all, and by loyal participation in the civic, economic and cultural life of the nation.

By discussion, talks and literature we seek to answer the inquiries of those who desire to obtain information about Christianity. We believe that we cannot refuse to do so, because we must share with everyone the light and joy of our faith.

Therefore we welcome as members of our churches those who ask to be admitted of their own free will and from strictly religious motives, and who have been under probation long enough to prove their sincerity, disinterestedness and ability to share the difficulties which are the lot of every religious minority.

This declaration expresses our conviction and our actual way of life, to both of which we wish to remain faithful.

The undersigned represent their various churches and dissociate themselves from any enterprise which individuals or groups may carry on otherwise than in the spirit of this declaration.

It is a true and splendid statement but unfortunately it is not much more than a clearing up of the abuses to which we have referred above. While in this first instance of a joint statement it might not have been possible to reach agreement on anything beyond the revoking of 'unacceptable missionary methods' there are signs in the various sections of the Church that something is being done to promote new attitudes and understanding of Jewry, Judaism and Israel. On the Roman Catholic side this has become evident in the efforts led by Father Bruno Hussar, centred in St Isaiah House, where several Dominican priests are devoting themselves to a serious study of a new understanding of Judaism. Dr Robert Lindsey, of the Baptist Convention in Israel, has not merely himself engaged in research in the Christian-Jewish relationship but has also greatly encouraged the holding of seminars at the Baptist Center in Petah Tiqva that has been largely concerned with these issues. In the spring of 1963 a Short Course in Jewish Studies was arranged under the auspices of the Anglican Jerusalem Archbishopric. Archbishop MacInnes, commending the report of this Course, wrote:

It promises well for the future if Christians are ready to seek a deeper understanding of the spiritual strivings of their Jewish neighbours and Jewish thinkers are ready to help them in their task.

The present writer, summing up the effect of this preliminary study wrote:

Where I think in some measure a new beginning can be seen among us is in the earnest search on the part of so many Christians in Israel for a new understanding of Judaism and what it has to say to us as Christians. When we came together in April we not only discovered that we shared this new awareness, but that we believed that it was Our Lord who

176

was demanding that we 'take off our shoes from off our feet', for when we genuinely seek to understand and study the Jewish Faith and People, we are on holy ground—God is present there and we need to approach humbly. If we can cultivate this new-born quest among us by being open-hearted as well as open-minded with each other, who can tell what God can do for all of us in the future?

All this and much more that is happening in the area of Christian-Jewish relations the world over only represents the first steps on what will inevitably be a long road, full of hazards, disappointments and set-backs, towards a full communal confrontation that is not content to be concerned with the mere periphery but courageously moves forward to a true meeting of hearts. This soul-to-soul encounter is not only a concern of Jews and Christians; rather it is a matter of God's total will for a world that has tired of the many voices of God's children and is fast drifting into militant unbelief. If Judaism and Christianity shirk the call of the present for a true 'face-lift', it may well be that neither will have a face in the world of tomorrow. It is not, however, the fear of 'no future' that should spur us on, but rather a discerning, a recognition that, on account of all that has happened and even more of what is happening in the present, it is God who is calling us to face each other in a new way that will at last remove the masks with which we have for so long deceived each other and will lead to that deep recognition and joy when we find in each other what God has entrusted to us both.

It is at the point of such a full and genuine encounter that we are led into the depth of the Christian Presence amid Judaism. The renowned second-century Christian

177

Apologists were able to perceive that wherever man discovered God there the Logos was present to guide him. Thus they could dare to claim all that pointed to God as being part of God's manifestation in Jesus. Can we be less daring in a similar age of crisis? Christians have always recognized that the Old Testament unfolds Jesus; it is, as Luther declared, 'Christ there in swaddling clothes'. Is it not possible that we have been blind to the further depths in which Jesus is made manifest in the travail and triumph of the Jewish people and faith throughout the ages? This is a dimension of the Lord Christ that Christians have yet to discover. But this cannot be a one-sided adventure. Already there are voices within Judaism that admit that there is deep failure in the Jewish evaluation of Jesus. Language is difficult at this point, for in the past any approach in this direction has inevitably meant absorption into a dominant Gentile Church. We have no other option but to express this in language of the past, though a genuinely new Jewish recognition of Jesus will undoubtedly be different from anything known to us so far. A Jew of the first century described this in a lyric that formed one of the earliest songs of Christian worship and found its way into the New Testament. It is cherished and used by Christians today the world over but its ethos remains essentially Jewish.

> This day, Master, thou givest thy servant his discharge in peace; now thy promise is fulfilled.
> For I have seen with mine own eyes the deliverance which thou hast made ready in full view of all the nations;
> A light that will be a revelation to the heathen, and glory to thy people Israel.

> (Luke 2.29-32, NEB)

Appendix I

*Statement by the Archbishop of Canterbury
issued from Lambeth Palace on 18 March 1964*
reproduced from *The Interpreter*, August 1964

It is always wrong when people try to lay the blame upon the Jews for the crucifixion of Jesus Christ. In the event the Roman Governor was no less responsible for what happened.

The important fact, however, is that the crucifixion was the clash between the Love of God and the sinfulness and selfishness of the whole human race. Those who crucified Christ are in the true mind of the Christian Church representatives of the whole human race, and it is for no one to point a finger of resentment at those who brought Jesus to his death, but rather to see the crucifixion as the divine judgment upon all humanity for choosing the ways of sin rather than the Love of God.

We all must see ourselves judged by the crucifixion of Christ.

signed
MICHAEL CANTUAR:

*Extract from The Declaration on the Relation of the Church
to Non-Christian Religions*

Officially promulgated in November 1965 at the final Session of the Vatican Ecumenical Council II. The section that specifically deals with the Church's attitude to Jewry and Judaism is the fourth and is entitled 'The Jewish Religion'.

As this Sacred Synod searches into the mystery of the Church, it remembers the bond that spiritually ties the people of the New Covenant to Abraham's stock.

In truth, the Church of Christ acknowledges that, according to God's saving design, the beginnings of her faith and her election are already found among the Patriarchs, Moses and the prophets. She professes that all who believe in Christ —Abraham's sons according to faith (cf. Gal. 3.7)—are included in the same Patriarch's call, likewise that the salvation of the Church is mysteriously foreshadowed by the chosen people's exodus from the land of bondage. The Church, therefore, cannot forget that she received the revelation of the Old Testament through the people with whom God in His ineffable mercy concluded the Ancient Covenant. Nor can she forget that she feeds upon the root of that cultivated olive tree into which the wild shoots of the Gentiles have been grafted (cf. Rom. 2.17-24). Indeed, the Church believes that by His cross Christ Our Peace reconciled Jews and Gentiles making both one in Himself (cf. Eph. 2.14-16).

The Church keeps ever in mind the words of the apostle about his kinsmen: 'theirs is the sonship and the glory and the covenants and the legislation and the worship and the promises; theirs are the fathers, and from them is the Christ according to the flesh' (cf. Rom. 9.4-5), the Son of the Virgin Mary. She also recalls that the Apostles, the Church's mainstay and pillars, as well as most of the early disciples who proclaimed Christ's Gospel to the world, sprang from the Jewish people.

As Holy Scripture testifies, Jerusalem did not recognize the time of her visitation (cf. Luke 19.44), nor did the Jews, for the most part, accept the Gospel; indeed many opposed its spreading (cf. Rom. 11.28). Nevertheless, according to the Apostle, God holds the Jews most dear for the sake of the Fathers: His gift and call are irrevocable (cf. Rom. 11.28-29; cf. *Constitution on the Church*, n. 16). In company with the

Appendix I

Prophets and the same Apostle, the Church awaits that day, known to God alone, on which all people will address the Lord in a single voice and 'serve him shoulder to shoulder' (Zeph. 3.9).

Since the spiritual patrimony common to Christians and Jews is thus of such magnitude, this Sacred Synod wants to foster and recommend a mutual knowledge and respect which is the fruit, above all, of biblical and theological studies as well as of fraternal dialogues.

Although the Jewish authorities and those who followed their lead pressed for the death of Christ (cf. John 19.6), nevertheless what happened to Christ in His passion cannot be attributed to all Jews, without distinction, then alive, nor to the Jews of today. Although the Church is the new people of God, the Jews should not be presented as rejected by God or accursed, as if this follows from the Holy Scriptures. May all see to it, then, that in catechetical work or in preaching the word of God they do not teach anything that is inconsistent with the truth of the Gospel and with the spirit of Christ.

Moreover, the Church, which rejects every persecution against any man, mindful of the common patrimony with the Jews and moved not by political reasons but by the Gospel's spiritual love, deplores hatred, persecutions, displays of anti-semitism, directed against Jews at any time and by anyone.

Besides, as the Church has always held and holds now, Christ underwent His passion and death freely, because of the sins of men and out of infinite love, in order that all may reach salvation. It is, therefore, the burden of the Church's preaching to proclaim the cross of Christ as the sign of God's all-embracing love and as the fountain from which every grace flows.

Appendix II

For Further Reading

Chapter 4 is not intended as an outline of the beliefs and aspirations of Judaism, but it is hoped that it will sufficiently stimulate the reader's interest and lead him to follow it up with some of the excellent expositions that are available in English. Out of the many that might be mentioned one can only select in an arbitrary manner. (For details see the Book List on pp. 191-93.) The following four are perhaps as representative a choice as possible. A great classic, by one of the foremost Christian scholars of Judaism of all time, George Foot Moore, is *Judaism in the First Centuries of the Christian Era*, a most authoritative and systematic presentation. In his own words its aim is

to represent Judaism in the centuries in which it assumed definitive form, as it represents itself in the tradition which it has always regarded as authentic.

The only drawback about this work is that it extends to two volumes with an additional one of notes! *Judaism, A Portrait*, by Leon Roth, is by contrast almost bedside reading. By this it is not meant to suggest that its scholarship is defective but rather that the artistic approach gives an easy flow and compelling interest to this work. Another attraction of this book is that it seems to have captured the very feel and atmosphere of Judaism. *Judaism and Modern Man* by Will Herberg is in the author's own words a 'confession of faith' with the particular value that it is given by a contemporary Jewish

182

Appendix II

theologian in North America who feels acutely the hazards and pressures of religion in the twentieth century. The rich variety of Jewish worship is most ably introduced for the Christian reader in a recent study by W. W. Simpson, *Jewish Prayer and Worship*.

Judaism has many facets. Judaism has a great history from the days of Abraham. Its literature is second to none and one part of it, the Old Testament, has found its place in the treasury of the two other great monotheistic faiths. Although philosophy and mysticism belong more properly to the Greeks, Judaism too has its fair share. All these are possible avenues to be explored and no doubt at every turn we should be confronted with some truth of Judaism that is of relevance to the Christian understanding of God, man, and the world. The most classical approach is undoubtedly the direct recourse to the normative Jewish sources of Talmud and Midrash. Few Christians realize that it is these writings that afford us the right clue to the Jewish interpretation of the Old Testament. Just as the New Testament is viewed in the Christian tradition as the right and natural development of the Old Testament, so in the Jewish tradition the same claim is made for Talmud and Midrash. This relationship was clearly recognized by two outstanding Christian Hebraists, Hermann Strack and Paul Billerbeck, who produced a monumental commentary on the New Testament composed of comparisons and parallels from the Talmud and Midrash. It is much to be regretted that Strack and Billerbeck's work in German has so far not been translated into any other language. In English among several works on similar lines none was quite as exhaustive as that of Strack and Billerbeck, though Claude Montefiore's two works *Commentary upon the Synoptic Gospels* and *Rabbinic Literature and Gospel Teaching*, and Israel Abraham's *Studies in Pharisaism and the Gospels* have the additional advantage of coming from Jewish scholars. A most recent work in this tradition of drawing out Jewish parallels

183

to the New Testament is W. D. Davies' careful study on *The Setting of the Sermon on the Mount*. This particular line of approach underlines the many similarities in thought and method between the New Testament and the rabbinical sources, but it also throws into open relief the crucial differences in the two sets of writings. It must be admitted that in the past Christian scholars have tended to view their excursions into Talmud and Midrash as a way of discovering similarities that underline the truth of the New Testament, a Jewish authentication of Christian truth. In fairness it should be added that this type of approach also led to a genuine Christian appreciation of the Talmud and Midrash that recaptured a most ancient Christian attitude characterized, as we noted in chapter two, by the phrase *Hebraica veritas*.

But this needs to be taken a step further. We might express this as not only seeking out those aspects of Talmud and Midrash that either corroborate or contradict Christian teaching and are thus directly related to Christianity but also facing the larger aspects of these writings which are not directly connected with Christian teaching. Perhaps we might underline this in a form of a hard question:

Has Rabbinic Judaism at the place of its most characteristic ethos and emphasis anything of value to impart to the Christian?

It is hoped that what has been attempted in chapter 4 will be of some help in providing an honest answer. It is often said that one who asks the right questions is more than halfway on the road to finding satisfying solutions. True as this may be (and it is of crucial importance in the present study), it can hardly be overemphasized that the rest of the way is by no means easy. Even when we are prepared to listen to Judaism in its normative expression, we are faced by the considerable hurdle of grappling with the original sources. The obstacles we face are not only the fact that they were written in Hebrew, but, even more, their idiom and their very size are forbidding to us moderns.

The **Mishnah**, about twice the size of the New Testament, has been translated into English by Herbert Danby. The Soncino Press has published an English translation of the **Babylonian Talmud** under the general editorship of Dr Epstein (London, 1935), and also seven volumes of the **Midrash Rabbah** under the general editorship of Freedman and Simon (London, 1939). When it is remembered that these volumes dwarf such forbidding collections as the complete works of the Ante-Nicene Fathers or the works of Martin Luther it will be appreciated that an anthology is desirable. Among the various anthologies *A Rabbinic Anthology* by C. G. Montefiore and H. H. Loewe is an outstanding achievement. It is perhaps the best anthology available in any language. Most of the quotations in chapter 4 are taken from this *Anthology* and perhaps this will stimulate the reader to pursue the treasures of this work for himself. It will be readily understood that rabbinic scholars are not exactly happy with anthologies or outline sketches on rabbinic themes, as they so easily impart a wrong perspective of the main interest and emphasis of the sources themselves. In part this can never be avoided, but all need not be lost if we bear in mind a basic differentiation of two types of rabbinic writing, that is, *halacha* and *haggada*, and exercise some patience with a few introductory remarks on the nature of Talmud and Midrash that may at least give us an inkling from where the various quotations in chapter 4 are derived.

The root meaning of *halacha* is 'to walk' and it carries with it the particular implication of direction; thus *halacha* is concerned with the authoritative direction and rule for the practice of religion. But this direction in religion was not primarily aimed at a clergy or restricted to particular sacred moments in the life of a laity, so that while *halacha* bears a certain resemblance to Canon Law, it is dissimilar from it. It aimed at covering all possible contingencies of life for the whole community of Israel. It is as much concerned with dietary and agricultural regulations as it is with rules for prayer; not only does it stipulate permissible degrees for marriage but it also lays down rules for sexual conduct within marriage, and so on. The root meaning of *haggada* is 'to expound or relate' and it refers to the exposition of and commentary on scripture, though at times the link between a *haggada* and scripture may become extremely tenuous. In the rabbinic scheme of things *halacha* is always primary and takes precedence over *haggada*. Not infrequently the rabbis compare *halacha* and *haggada* as wine to water. In modern parlance one might say that *halacha* is the charter of rabbinic religion, *haggada* is the mere preamble. Yet the relation was more complex than this. There are times when it is difficult to say precisely where *halacha* ends and *haggada* begins, often there is an interpenetration of the one upon the other. Claude Montefiore admits that his *Anthology* is almost exclusively occupied with *haggada*. This is hardly avoidable, when one is primarily concerned with a description of rabbinic religion rather than with directions for its practice. The only way to redress this lopsidedness would be not merely to study *halacha* but to practise it. If one's study has largely to be limited to anthologies and rabbinic concepts, all need not be lost provided that we at least keep in mind the essential framework of *halacha* in which the religious and moral teaching of the rabbis, be it by anecdote, homily, parable, allegory, legend or the non-legal interpretation of scripture, essentially belongs.

As to the composite nature of Talmud and Midrash we have already noted that the Talmud is made up of Mishnah and Gemara and that the Tosefta is a parallel work to the Mishna. The rabbinic literature loosely described by the umbrella term of *Midrash* is if anything more composite and complicated than the Talmud. The essential meaning of *Midrash* is that of 'searching out', and this is directly applied to the meaning of scripture, so that broadly speaking Midrash is a rabbinical commentary on scripture. There are a considerable number of Midrashic collections, some as early as the Mishnah, many are of the same period (late sixth century) as the completion of the Babylonian Talmud, while others are as late as the eleventh or twelfth century. By far the most competent and lucid explanation of this involved literature is that by Hermann L. Strack in his *Introduction to Talmud and Midrash*. For our purpose it would be sufficient to mention the most outstanding of these collections, from many of which quotations are made in the fourth chapter. Midrashic works are essentially of two kinds, homiletical and expositional. The **Homiletical Midrashim** (plural of Midrash) follow the order of various Jewish selections of scripture on a cyclical basis for Sabbaths and Feasts. It is rather like a commentary on the Epistles and Gospels for a specific period of the Church's year or a commentary based on the order of a lectionary. The **Expositional Midrashim** follow roughly the order of the particular scripture on which they are commenting and so approximate to the usual pattern of a Christian biblical commentary.

The outstanding Homiletical Midrashim are the Pesiktas and the Tanchuma. There are two Pesiktas, the primary one the **Pesikta de Rab Kahana** which is often simply referred to as **The Pesikta**. It is composed of homilies for festivals and special Sabbaths: its date is about 700. The other work is known as **Pesikta Rabbati** and is similar in structure and content only considerably larger and so is often referred to as the **Great Pesikta**. Its date is probably about 900. The **Tanchuma** (also known as *Yalemmedenu Rabbenu* from an oft-repeated introductory phrase meaning 'May our master instruct us') is an homiletic midrash on the Sabbath lections in the whole Pentateuch. The name derives from the opening of several discourses with the phrase 'so did R. Tanchuma

bar Abba introduce the discourse' or possibly from a foundation for these homilies laid by this rabbi of the mid-fourth
century. Four more Homiletic Midrashim related to Exodus,
Leviticus, Numbers and Deuteronomy should be mentioned.
These and some other commentaries are commonly designated
as *Rabba*, literally 'much' or 'many' and meaning in this
connection 'a great collection'. It is perhaps similar to our use
of 'the Great' in connection with names of churches which in
the first instance was used to distinguish them from another
smaller 'the less'. The **Midrash Exodus Rabba** has fifty-two
sections in which the first fourteen are a running commentary
on the various verses for a particular occasion and the rest is
composed of homilies on the first verses of the passages dealt
with in the first section. Its date is about 900. The **Midrash
Leviticus Rabba** consists of thirty-seven sections, it is the
oldest of the present group of Midrashim, coming from about
the same time as the Pesikta. Its special interest is that in
seven of its sections it follows a different division of scripture
for Sabbath readings. It is also noted for its great use of proverbs. The **Midrash Numbers Rabba** is composed of twenty-
three sections which fall into two quite different parts. In the
first fourteen sections are a combination of homiletical and
expositional material closely placed together so that the result
is almost a running commentary on Numbers 1-7. Sections
fifteen to twenty-three are more strictly homiletical and
cover roughly the annual cycle of Sabbath readings that are
taken from Numbers 8-25. Its date is thought to be as late as
the twelfth century though the second part is largely dependent on the Tanchuma and so of course much earlier. The
Midrash Deuteronomy Rabba is composed of eleven sections
based on the annual cycle for Sabbath readings, but in these
sections there are twenty-seven homilies which are based on
the text of a triennial cycle of sabbath readings. There are
several additions and fragments of which the most noted is
said to be based on the **Midrash on the Passing Away of**

Moses. The date of this is about nine hundred. It should be mentioned that these four Midrashim are often referred to by the names of the Hebrew title of the Book of the Bible on which they are based.

The **Expositional Midrashim** approximate to the traditional Christian biblical commentary and are thus for the Christian far easier to understand. By far the most important is the work on Genesis, the **Midrash Genesis Rabba**. This is practically a running commentary on Genesis and the greater part of it is of the Amoraic period. A widely held tradition ascribes the composition of this Midrash to a noted Palestinian Amora, named Osiah or Hoshaiah, from about the mid-third century. The **Midrash Lamentations Rabba** is a very similar work to that of Genesis and some think not much older, though Zunz, a great nineteenth-century Jewish student of the Midrashim, places it as late as the second half of the seventh century. It undoubtedly originated from a custom of basing homilies on Lamentations on the anniversary of the fall of Jerusalem. Another set of Midrashic collections sometimes referred to as Rabbot (plural of Rabba) are expositional commentaries on the Song of Songs (our Song of Solomon), Ruth, Ecclesiastes and Esther; these are predominantly of late composition. There is also a **Midrash on the Psalms** which is of a markedly composite nature, with frequent repetitions. Strack thinks that this Midrash may well illustrate the way in which homilies and exegetical material were collected together until there developed a fairly extensive commentary on a whole biblical book. As may be expected, this Midrash is most difficult to date and in all probability is as late as the twelfth century.

There is another group of Midrashaic collections which on account of both their early composition and difficulty of placing in either the Homiletical or Expositional group are treated separately. They are termed the **Tannaitic Midrashim** and are composed of three collections, the **Mekilta, Sifra**, and

Sifre. The **Sifra**, literally 'the book', a Midrash on Leviticus, is so named, as it was customary in the rabbinical schools to commence the study of the Torah with the third volume of the Pentateuch. Its other title, *Torat Kohanim*, the Law of the Priests, suggests its contents of legal homilies for priests based on Leviticus. It is similar to Canon Law. The designation **Sifre** may be taken as almost a general term for ancient legal Midrashim. The best known of such works is a commentary on the legal section of Deuteronomy (12-26) known as Sifre Deuteronomy. There is also a Sifre on Numbers and the traces of such a work on Leviticus. The **Mekilta** on Exodus was at one time classed as a Sifre on Exodus but is now generally referred to as the Mekilta. It is predominantly like a Sifre, a legal commentary, but it has considerable expositional material, so that it reads almost like a running commentary on the legal chapters of Exodus (12-23). Besides this it is the oldest rabbinical commentary on Exodus and a great favourite in anthologies. There is yet one other Midrashic work that must be mentioned; it is the **Yalkut**. This is almost entirely a mediaeval conflation (about the thirteenth century) of earlier Midrashim; its great distinction is that it is a running, though very uneven, commentary on the whole of the Old Testament.

From this brief introduction to the Talmud and Midrash one thing at least should be clear and that is the very marked difference between the composition of these writings and the systematic theological treatises of the Christian Fathers. The rabbis of the Talmudic era did not produce a single volume of dogmatic theology, simply because they were not theologians in the way that we apply that term to professional Christian thinkers, writers and teachers; but they were theologians in the classical sense of that term in that they taught men about God. They were primarily students of the Torah who out of a continuing discussion of their religion taught and directed their community. While the rabbis steered clear of systematized thought and were not preoccupied with 'theological terms' or 'word books' they did of course develop particular methods of study and the use of special terms which in the course of time have been loaded with significance. It is however almost invidious to try and determine any priority among such terms.

The rabbis might agree that *Shema*, *Shechina*, *Torah* and *Mitzvot* are primary to their thinking. They would undoubtedly disagree with the suggestion that the many other terms excluded from this list, and in particular *Kavana*, *Teshuva* and *Kiddush ha Shem*, were not of fundamental importance to their thinking. It can only be hoped that the outline study of the first terms in chapter 4 will so excite the reader's enthusiasm for what the rabbis have to say that he will follow up the other terms for himself in the works quoted.

Book List

General

Will Herberg, *Judaism and Modern Man*, Farrar Straus and Young, New York, 1951

G. F. Moore, *Judaism in the First Centuries of the Christian Era*, 3 vols., Harvard University Press, Cambridge, Mass., 1927-30

Leon Roth, *Judaism, A Portrait*, Faber and Faber, London, 1960

W. W. Simpson, *Jewish Prayer and Worship*, SCM Press, London, 1965

For chapter 1

Josef Bor, *The Terezin Requiem*, Eng. trans. by Edith Pargeter, Heinemann, London, 1963

James Parkes, *Antisemitism*, Vallentine Mitchell, London, 1963

Joshua Trachtenberg, *The Devil and the Jews*, Yale University Press, New Haven, and Oxford University Press, 1943

191

For chapter 2

Israel Abrahams, *Studies in Pharisaism and the Gospels*, Cambridge University Press, 1924

Gregory Baum, *The Jews and the Gospel*, Bloomsbury Publishing Co., London, 1961

David Daube, *The New Testament and Rabbinic Judaism*, Athlone Press, London, 1956

W. D. Davies, *Paul and Rabbinic Judaism*, SPCK, London, 1948

W. D. Davies, *The Setting of the Sermon on the Mount*, Cambridge University Press, 1964

Travers Herford, *The Pharisees*, Allen and Unwin, London, 1924

Claude Montefiore, *Commentary upon the Synoptic Gospels*, Macmillan, London, 1909

Claude Montefiore, *Rabbinic Literature and Gospel Teaching*, Macmillan, London, 1930

C. F. D. Moule, *The Birth of the New Testament*, A. & C. Black, London, 1962

Hans Schoeps, *Paul: The Theology of the Apostle in the Light of Jewish Religious History*, Eng. trans. by Harold Knight, Lutterworth Press, London, 1961

Paul Winter, *On the Trial of Jesus*, Walter de Gruyter, Berlin, 1961

For chapter 3

Max Dimmont, *The Jews, God and History*, W. H. Allen, London, 1964

Morris Goldstein, *Jesus in the Jewish Tradition*, Macmillan, New York, 1950

Travers Herford, *Christianity in Talmud and Midrash*, Williams and Norgate, London, 1903

Hans Schoeps, *The Jewish-Christian Argument*, Eng. trans. by David E. Green, publ. Holt, Rinehart and Winston, New York, 1963

Appendix II

For chapter 4

The Mishnah, English translation by Herbert Danby, Clarendon Press, Oxford, 1933

Claude Montefiore and H. H. Loewe, *A Rabbinic Anthology*, Macmillan, London, 1938; reissued by Meridian Books, New York 1960

Hermann Strack, *Introduction to Talmud and Midrash*, Eng. trans. by the Jewish Publication Society of America, Philadelphia, 1931

For chapter 5

Jews and Christians, ed. G. A. F. Knight, Westminster Press, Philadelphia, 1965

James Parkes, *The Foundations of Judaism and Christianity*, Vallentine Mitchell, London, 1960

A. Lukyn Williams, *Adversus Judaeos*, Cambridge University Press, 1935

Glossary

Amora A sage of the latter Talmudic era. Plural, *Amoraim*.

Eretz Yisrael The Land of Israel.

Gemara The second section of the Talmud, virtually a commentary on the first and more authoritative section, the Mishnah.

Haggada The root meaning is to 'expound' or 'relate' and it refers to the exposition of and commentary on scripture, though at times the direct link of a *haggada* with scripture may be extremely tenuous. *Haggada* is also the name of the traditional liturgy used for the Seder.

Halacha The root meaning is 'to walk' and it carries with it the particular implication of direction. Thus *halacha* is concerned with authoritative direction and rule for the practice of religion.

Kavana Rabbinic word for 'concentration' and 'attention'.

Kavod Hebrew word for 'glory'.

Kibbutz Modern Hebrew word for a collective settlement in Israel.

Kiddush ha Shem Literally 'the Sanctification of the Name' which emphasizes Israel's responsibility toward God as the trustee of his reputation in the world.

Lishma A rabbinic word for 'motive' and 'intention'.

Malkut Shamayim Literally the 'Kingdom of Heaven' but more properly 'God's Kingly Rule' which expresses the rabbis' great stress on God's sovereignty.

Mezuza Literally 'doorpost', but refers specifically to the glass, wood or metal case fixed on the doorpost containing the first two paragraphs of the Shema (Deut. 6.4-9 and 11.13-21).

194

Glossary

Medinat Yisrael The State of Israel.

Midrash The root meaning is that of 'searching out' and this is directly applied to the meaning of scripture. Thus broadly speaking a midrash is a rabbinical commentary on scripture. The midrashim (plural) form in some sense a parallel set of writings to the Talmud.

Mishna The first and most authoritative section of the Talmud completed by the third century.

Mitzva Literally a 'commandment', but referring specifically to religious injunctions and obligations and more generally to any good deed. Plural, *mitzvot*.

Pessach The Feast of Passover.

Purim Mainly a children's festival based on the story of the Book of Esther, it has now developed in Israel into a carnival.

Rosh ha Shana Literally 'Head of the Year' and hence the name for the Jewish New Year's Day.

Seder The beautiful family meal and service that initiates the Feast of Passover.

Shabbat The Hebrew word for Saturday, the weekly Jewish day of rest.
Erev shabbat the 'Eve of the Sabbath', is Friday evening.

Shavuot Literally 'weeks' and hence the name for the Feast of Weeks or Pentecost.

Shechina A rabbinic word for the concept of God's presence.

Shema Literally 'Hear!'; the first word of the great Jewish affirmation of monotheism found in Deut. 6.4.

Shikun Apartment building or block of flats in Israel. Plural, *shikunim*.

Sidur A Jewish prayer book.

Succot From *succa*, a 'covering', and hence the name of the Feast of Booths or Tabernacles.

Talmud This is an umbrella term covering the normative rabbinic writings composed of the Mishna and Gemara. It exists in two versions, the Jerusalem Talmud completed by the fifth century and the Babylonian Talmud completed by the sixth century.

Tanna A sage of the Mishnaic period. Plural, *Tannaim.*

Teshuva Hebrew word for 'repentance'.

Torah Technically this refers to the Pentateuch but pragmatically it covers the whole area of Bible, revelation, and religious direction. It is the expressed will of God, for Israel, as at first given by Moses and later expounded and extended by the rabbis. *Simhat Torah*, literally 'The Joy of the Torah' is the name of the anniversary Festival for the giving of the Law.

Tosefta A parallel work to the Mishna which was not included in the Talmud.

Ulpan Adult Hebrew language course. Plural, *ulpanim.*

Yirat Shamayim Literally the 'fear of Heaven', stressing the awe and deference that is God's due.

Yishuv Literally 'dwelling', referring specifically to the resettlement of Jews in Israel.

Yom Kippur The most solemn day in the Jewish year, namely the Day of Atonement.

Q. 8.31 – what does this reference mean?

162, ✱163
165, 167, 169